Ombré Quilts

6 COLORFUL PROJECTS

Jennifer Sampou

C&T PUBLISHING

Text and photography copyright © 2019 by Jennifer Sampou

Photography and artwork copyright © 2019 by C&T Publishing, Inc.

Publisher: Amy Barrett-Daffin

Creative Director: Gailen Runge

Acquisitions Editor: Roxane Cerda

Managing/Developmental Editor: Liz Aneloski

Technical Editor: Debbie Rodgers

Cover/Book Designer: April Mostek

Production Coordinator: Zinnia Heinzmann

Production Editor: Jennifer Warren

Illustrator: Valyrie Gillum

Photo Assistant: Rachel Holmes

Style photography by Jennifer Sampou unless otherwise noted; instructional photography by Kelly Burgoyne and Rachel Holmes of C&T Publishing, Inc., unless otherwise noted

Fabric-swatch photography courtesy of Robert Kaufman Fabrics

Published by C&T Publishing, Inc., P.O. Box 1456, Lafayette, CA 94549

Library of Congress Cataloging-in-Publication Data

Names: Sampou, Jennifer, 1966- author.

Title: Ombre quilts : 6 colorful projects / Jennifer Sampou.

Description: Lafayette, CA : C&T Publishing, Inc., [2019]

Identifiers: LCCN 2019019721 | ISBN 9781617459139 (softcover)

Subjects: LCSH: Quilting--Patterns.

Classification: LCC TT835 .S2613 2019 | DDC 746.46/041--dc23

LC record available at https://lccn.loc.gov/2019019721

Printed in the USA

10 9 8 7 6 5 4 3

Dedication

To my family, from the roots up:

Mom and Dad, you've always been my North Star.

My siblings, XOXO. Lucky me!

My husband, you are the most ombré of hombres. Forever and always.

My boys—Dad and I are so blessed to share this remarkable journey with you three.

Acknowledgments

Ombré Quilts would not be possible without the team effort of so many people, both listed and unlisted. For that collaboration and effort, I am deeply grateful.

Thanks to my C&T Publishing family for all the hard work and making it fun: Liz Aneloski, Amy Barrett-Daffin, Kelly Burgoyne, Tristan Gallagher (always and forever!), Zinnia Heinzmann, April Mostek, Debbie Rodgers, Gailen Runge, and Jennifer Warren. Nothing like a deadline to keep the BERNINA humming!

Thank you to my feisty, cheerful mother-in-law and shop owner, Carolie Hensley, for supporting me and my career since day one and buying *all* my fabrics.

My gratitude to my lifelong friend Amanda Houston, artist extraordinaire, who's artistic beauty knows no bounds.

Marcella Austenfeld, I cherish our friendship and the undeniable fact that you are the fork to my salad.

My appreciation to the Robert Kaufman family for bringing my fabric designs to market—with a special shout-out to Ken Kaufman, Jane Wilkings, and Sarah Grubb for saying, "*Yes!*" to SKY collection, working through every color combination of SKY, and providing *all* the fabric *way early* to make these quilts.

To the Hello Stitch crew, who support our network of makers and quilters via your studio and services.

My sincere thanks to designers Vanessa Christenson, Nicole Daksiewicz, and Malka Dubrawsky, as well as Hoffman Fabrics.

It takes a bee! I am grateful for talented makers Jenny Lyon, Jocelyn Marzan, Ashleigh Pevey, Kristen Takakuwa, color maven Joen Wolfrom, and Jess Zeigler. Without your assistance, I would have never finished this book nor had as much fun doing it!

Finally, I have to again acknowledge my husband, Todd Hensley, for the hours and hours of patient help. You are the peanut butter to my jelly.

Contents

The Projects

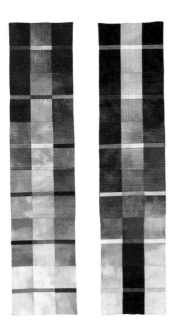
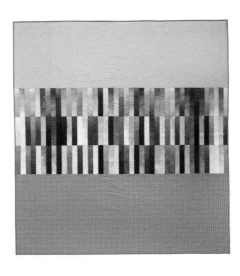

*I*ntroduction

For my thirtieth year of being a professional designer, I decided to write a quilt book in conjunction with designing a line of fabric by picking a favorite topic: Ombré. This style is all the rage, and it has made its way into every visual industry from hair to wallpaper. It's here to stay. As a trend lover, I have enjoyed watching this wave crescendo, and our very own quilt industry has begun to embrace ombré fabrics, which is so inspirational!

Hand dyers have always offered up their version of gradient dip-dyed beauties. With digital printing, our printing possibilities and fabric color options have exploded. It's evident from internet searches of ombré fabrics that we are the recipients of such gorgeous gradations of color and texture. So dig in with me! I have designed some very approachable designs with stunning effects. Learn how to use these "prints" and come to trust me when I say they will delight you (even if you don't know exactly how to use them when you begin). It's time to embrace the rich variations of these fabrics we have at our fingertips. Go on … cut into, play around with, and sew that stack you have been petting; ombré fabrics make the most delicious quilts. I have set up the projects starting with a gorgeous table topper and an easy precut yellow quilt sure to light your ombré fire!

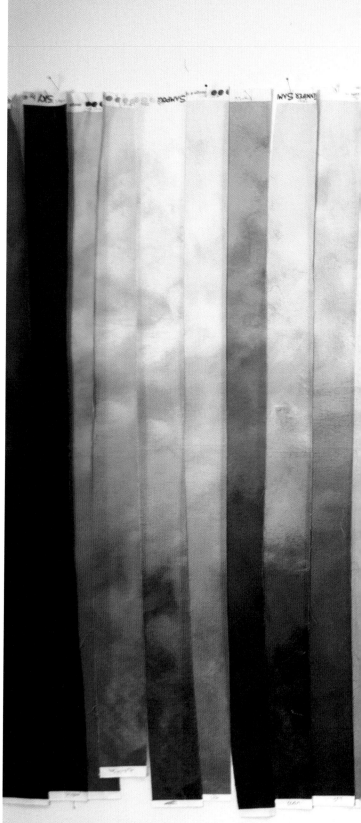

Photo by Todd Hensley

Ombré Fabrics
A Thousand Colors at Your Fingertips

WHAT IS AN OMBRÉ?

Ombré is the French word for color that is shaded or graduated in tone or hue. It historically referred to fashion clothing, like a silk gown that has a rich rose hem and gradually lightens to a pale pink bodice. There are endless variations of how ombré fabrics can be painted, screen-printed, dipped, or colored. Further, the technique can vary from superfine blending to bold and textural gradation. As long as the final outcome results in a change in value and/or color, drawing your eye through a shaded effect, it is considered an ombré.

Quilters have successfully created ombré quilts by piecing entire color families of cotton solids together or by using hand-dyed ombré fabrics. Now we can print hundreds of colors in one yard of fabric; use a grouping of these ombrés and you have a thousand colors at your fingertips!

Ombré's popularity and reinventions have cycled once again and we currently see fresh, modern interpretations. One thing is for sure: Ombrés are eye-catching, gorgeous, and often mimic nature, whether it's the inside of a seashell; the shading of a flower petal; a distant, layered mountain range; or the grandeur of a dawn sky.

Note ▶ Synonyms for Ombré: *Graduated color blends, variegated, color gradient, color progression, tie-dye, dip-dye, painted blend, blended, rainbow, transitional color, and more! For the purpose of clarity, I will use the word* **ombré** *throughout this book.*

Photo by Ruth Black/Shutterstock.com

Photo by Africa Studio/Shutterstock.com

Shimmer On fabric by Jennifer Sampou
for Robert Kaufman Fabrics

1. Photo by
Jennifer Sampou

2. *Modern Handcraft
Hexie Quilt*, by
Nicole Daksiewicz

Photo by
Nicole Daksiewicz

3. *Lilac Quilt*, by
Malka Dubrawsky

Photo by
Annie Winsett

4. Photo by
Photographee.eu/
Shutterstock.com

WHY I LOVE OMBRÉ FABRICS

When I show my work, the quilts often elicit oohs and aahs from the audience; they want to know my process and the secrets of what makes a gorgeous quilt. Capturing light is not necessarily a conscious goal quilters identify when they set out to sew a quilt. It tends to be a discussion and a thought map about color and pattern. However, over the past several years, many of the quilts I have made begin with my primary intention to capture light, reflect light, or bounce lights and darks around on a quilt. This in turn creates glow, depth, richness, and contrast. It helps move your eye around the quilt, creating interest and harmony. But it all boils down to light, or the lack of it, which is another way of defining value.

The relationship of color—and especially value—matter. Are they bright to dirty or calm to energetic? How do these colors look next to those? Are there enough darks and lights? Choosing a palette that supports a main color theme, supported by subsets of those colors, is how you build a robust quilt-fabric palette. I am going to share how I do this by using ombré fabrics, because they make it much easier to be successful. Why? Because with ombrés, you get an entire range of a color, mixed and printed in just 1 yard of fabric. You don't need 20–30 separate pieces of fabric to achieve variety when a few ombrés will do the trick.

Heading for the Wind, pastel art by Amanda Houston

Photo by Amanda Houston (amandahouston.com)

With my SKY collection for Robert Kaufman Fabrics, I have already delineated and broken down what makes a gorgeous ombré. This expression is lyrical and organic. You won't get a "perfect seven hues in seven values" kind of palette but a moody range with lots of darks to whisper lights, a dash of the dulls, as well as rich, vibrant jewel tones and energetic brights. Cut it up and sew it back together to discover all the wonders that can be achieved! Variety happens automatically and just ten fabrics will yield hundreds of colors. It's visual poetry!

A fun part of working with ombré fabrics is the delight of what actually unfolds when you cut them up and sew them back together. We can't see all possibilities, like one might when working with solid fabrics or petite prints. We won't know what will bloom until we are in the midst of cutting, placing, creating, and combining. This on-the-fly discovery is what makes it magic and the reason I love working with them (and you will, too!).

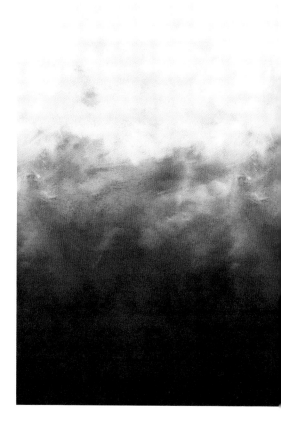

I hope this book brings you more awareness of how to harness the beauty of light by using ombré fabrics. Walk into a shop and unroll a bolt to see for yourself. Let's dive in! Use ombré fabrics and start to play. I think you will love the way your heart skips when the captivating combinations of simply sewn and pressed seams result in a dynamic block and a stunning quilt.

CREATING OMBRÉ FABRICS

When I design a new collection, I use watercolor paints, gouache, pen and ink, encaustic, mixed media, acrylics, or whatever I need to get the look I want. However, due to limitations of cotton screen-printing technology, I have been limited to the use of sixteen colors per design. Digital printing, which is a newer process, is becoming more popular due to its enhanced quality and affordability. It offers *limitless detailed colors* on one yard of fabric. This recent printing breakthrough gives us affordable and stunning quilting cotton that has never before been possible.

My artwork is processed by computer and printed directly onto cotton cloth. It's somewhat like your home printer, but 100% cotton cloth is the substrate and high-quality, reactive dyes are the inks used. The digital printer does not use individual screens for each unique color, as in screen-printed fabrics, but instead prints thousands of tiny droplets of color. Digital printing has been used for polyester, LYCRA, and other man-made textiles for years and has provided stunning effects, but for cotton it had been cost prohibitive or resulted in dull colors.

During a design meeting, Robert Kaufman Fabrics shared with me the range of newly offered digital-printing capabilities. I could barely contain my enthusiasm. Clouds have been a lifelong inspiration to me—something I aspire to capture on textiles. Before I could sleep that night, I had a chat with an artist friend, Amanda Houston, and asked her to school me in creating dramatic skies with pastel sticks. Soon I was drawing skies in my studio and amassing piles of pictures of inspirational clouds. My SKY collection of 30 unique ombré fabrics ranges from predawn through midnight. I worked with Robert Kaufman Studio to create these prints that capture all types of weather patterns imagined and witnessed, beholding the tremendous light and color above us.

TYPES OF OMBRÉ FABRICS

Ombrés come in a variety of layouts, color ranges, repeat sizes, panels, continuous printings, and more. The most common are explored here. Expect variations—we have done our best to represent SKY fabrics as accurately as possible.

Full-Range Ombrés

The fabrics appear darker at one selvage and lighter at the other, fading gradually across the entire 44″ width of the fabric. Presented here and used for the projects in this book are fabrics from my SKY collection. The photos provided are courtesy of Robert Kaufman Fabrics.

Sky

Storm

Powder

Azure

Ocean

Prairie Sky

Evening

Turkish Sea

Tornado

Sea Glass

Shadow

Fog

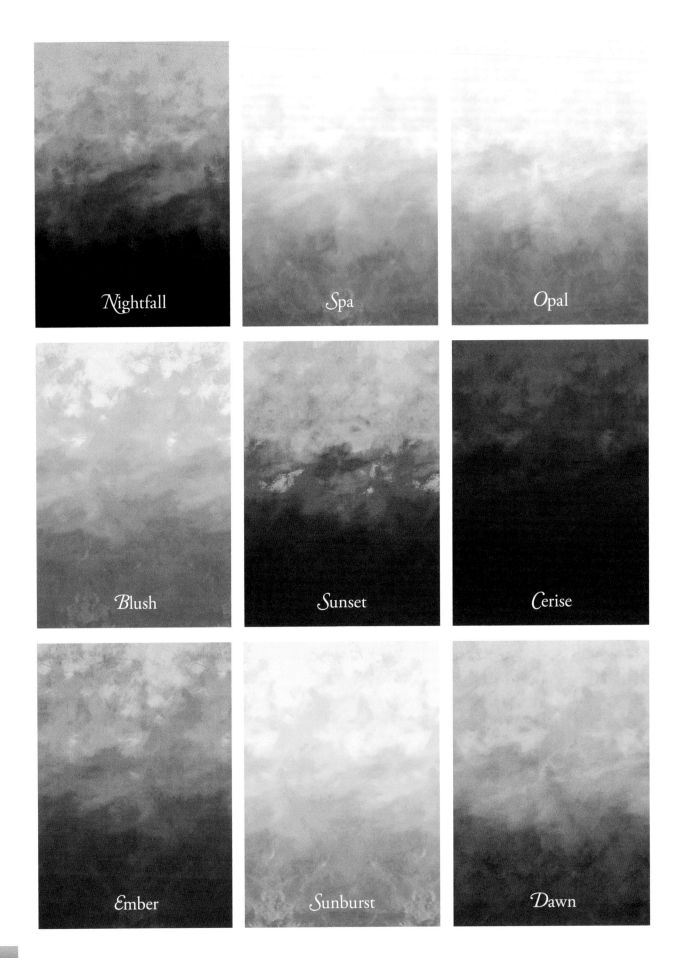

Nightfall

Spa

Opal

Blush

Sunset

Cerise

Ember

Sunburst

Dawn

Sundance

Mist

Noble Purple

Atmosphere

Haze

Midnight

Heather

Celestial

Cloud

There are many other gorgeous full-range ombré fabrics available for quilters:

Fresh Hues Ombre collection from Robert Kaufman Fabrics

Patina Handpaints Ombre by Lunn Studios
for Robert Kaufman Fabrics

Mirrored Ombrés

These fabrics are darker at both selvages and graduate to light in the center of the fabric, or, conversely, are lighter at both selvages and graduate to darker in the center.

Black & White collection by Jennifer Sampou for Robert Kaufman Fabrics

Ombre Confetti Metallic by V and Co. for Moda Fabrics + Supplies

Photo by Vanessa Christenson

Everything Else

The list of available ombré fabrics goes beyond the full-range and mirrored ombrés to include panels, bias, circular, rainbow, bubble texture, dot, batik, floral, hand dyed, striped, and more.

Supernova panel from Hoffman California Fabrics

Dream Big Floral panel from Hoffman California Fabrics

WHICH OMBRÉ FABRICS SHOULD I BUY?

Buy the ones you love and can't resist! With an amazing array of colors in just a few printed yards, it's so exciting to be able to use these ombrés to make cotton quilts. Buy a range of colors from light to dark. To make the quilts in this book, I used my SKY collection and incorporated a few Kona Cottons and my Yarn Dyes collection. You can adapt any type of ombré fabric you have and get your own unique look with wonderful results. You may need to vary the cutting format or options with certain mirrored ombrés. The options for cutting up circular or bias-type ombrés are not covered in this book, but you can play with these and cut areas you want to use.

CUTTING YOUR OMBRÉ FABRICS

Because ombré fabrics change throughout the length and width, thinking about all the options of *how* you can cut them up and use them is something to consider before you just stack and whack it. Granted, I am not going to judge you if that's what you want to do—go for it! I love that kind of "with abandon," risky-yet-brave approach to making. However, if you want to have a bit more control over your results, here are some ways to cut up these ombrés to capture areas you want to highlight.

Cross grain: Cutting across the ombré, selvage to selvage, gives you the maximum range of color transition.

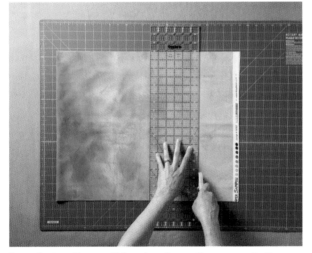

Lengthwise: Cut parallel to the selvages if you want similar colors in larger or longer pieces.

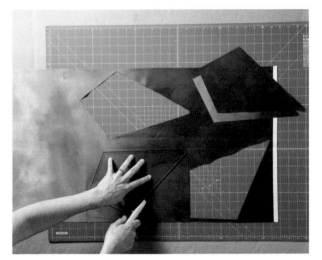

Fussy cutting: Isolate areas of the ombré you want to use.

For most of my projects, I start by layering a few fabrics, knowing that one end was light and the other dark. When I layer the fabrics, I am more open to a variety of results. I pick my favorite parts to put into the quilt, while some are left as scraps for another day. When I want to highlight specific areas of my favorite part of a fabric and *be sure* to get them in a certain place, I fussy cut each piece with no layering. Decide what is best for you and approach your fabric cutting accordingly.

The Projects

Every ombré referred to in the following projects is from my SKY collection (see Full-Range Ombrés, page 12). With these references at your fingertips, you can substitute other ombré fabrics, whether they are your own hand-dyes or other manufactured prints. Simply evaluate the palette; then gather your stack of fabrics!

Modern Madras
Reversible Table Runner

Finished runner: 72″ × 16½″

The Modern Madras Reversible Table Runner is a simple study in ombrés. This is a beginner project because you limit your choice to just three or four fabrics per side. It's very manageable and has fantastic results. All your friends and family will want you to make one for them! I chose a warm palette on one side and a cool one for the other.

Quilted by Ashleigh Pevey

Warm-palette side

Cool-palette side

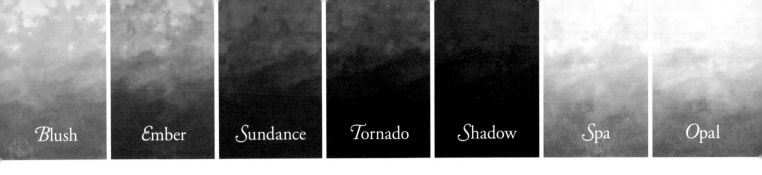

Blush | Ember | Sundance | Tornado | Shadow | Spa | Opal

MATERIALS

Note *Warm colors tend to be from yellow to orange to red hues. Cool colors tend to be from purple to blue to green hues.*

Warm side

Blush, Ember, and Sundance:
½ yard each

Cool side

Tornado, Shadow, and Spa:
½ yard each

Opal: ¼ yard

Thin cotton batting: 72″ × 16½″

DESIGNING THE TABLE RUNNER

The warm side of the table runner blends from lights to darks, with a lighter madras transparency down the middle of the runner. You will have extra blocks to play with and narrow bars to choose between. This is where you can easily exercise your color and value exploration with ombré fabrics. Because this is a small project, it should not be overwhelming nor terribly time-consuming.

The cool side flips the center ombré to be opposite of the edges, which creates a bit more drama. This palette reminds me of the tide pools in Mendocino, California, where the cold waters make your feet ache but shimmering bits of opalescence amongst the cool greens and aquas keep you searching.

TIP You can repeat the pattern five more times and make a lap quilt with each row being a different color story!

CUTTING

Cutting is based on 42″ usable width of fabric (WOF).

Warm side

Cut 2 strips 6″ × WOF each of Blush, Ember, and Sundance; subcut each strip into 6 squares 6″ × 6″.

Cut 1 strip 1½″ × WOF each of Blush, Ember, and Sundance; subcut each strip into 6 rectangles 1½″ × 6″.

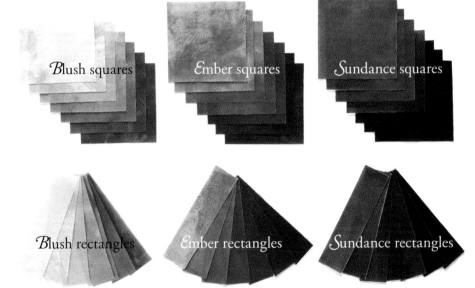

Blush squares   Ember squares   Sundance squares

Blush rectangles   Ember rectangles   Sundance rectangles

Cool side

Cut 2 strips 6″ × WOF each of Tornado, Shadow, and Spa; subcut each strip into 6 squares 6″ × 6″.

Cut 2 strips 1½″ × WOF of Opal; subcut each strip into 7 rectangles 1½″ × 6″.

Cut 1 strip 1½″ × WOF of Spa; subcut into 4 rectangles 1½″ × 6″.

CONSTRUCTION

Warm Side

1. Arrange your squares and rectangles from light to dark. Refer to the warm-side photo (page 24).

 TIP Make one block at a time, returning it back into your layout, so you don't get them mixed up.

2. For the outer-row blocks, sew a 6″ × 6″ square to each side of a 1½″ × 6″ rectangle, right sides together. Press the seams to the rectangle. Make 12.

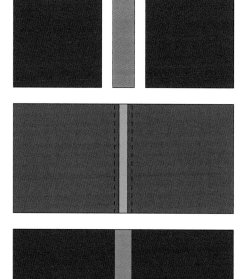

3. For the long center-row blocks, sew a 6″ × 6″ square to each side of a 1½″ × 6″ rectangle, right sides together. Press the seams away from the rectangle. Make 6.

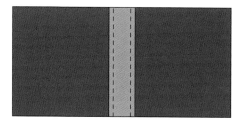

4. Choose the 3 blocks in the first unit and sew them together into a unit, in the order shown. Press the seams open.

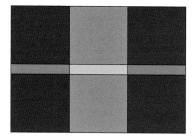

5. Repeat Step 4 to make 6 units that contain 3 blocks each. Be sure to keep them in the correct order.

6. Sew the units together. Press the seams open.

Warm side

Cool Side

Repeat Warm Side, Steps 1–6 (page 23 and above) using the cool-side fabrics.

Cool side

FINISHING

For a table topper, I prefer the look of an envelope-style finish rather than quilt binding. It's cleaner, and I just tie off the quilt threads and tuck them into the seam to bury them.

1. Place the warm and cool sides right sides together, matching the seams. Sew together with a ¼″ seam allowance around 3 sides, leaving one short end open.

2. Trim off the triangle corners. Spray baste the batting and place it on one side. Reverse out and smooth the table runner on both sides.

3. Fold ¼″ in on the open short side and stitch closed.

4. With your domestic machine, matchstick quilt for a professional finish. The matchstick finish washes great and looks better with use—and you know this will get lots of use!

Yellow Bars Quilt

Finished quilt: 84½″ × 89½″

Yellow Bars is a perfect quilt project for beginners wanting to work with an entire range of ombré fabrics. I used all 30 ombré fabrics of my SKY collection (see Full-Range Ombrés, page 12, for photos of these fabrics). This quilt uses 2½″-wide precut strips, making it an easy and fast project that proves how beautifully these fabrics work together. You pick your favorite color for the top and bottom field.

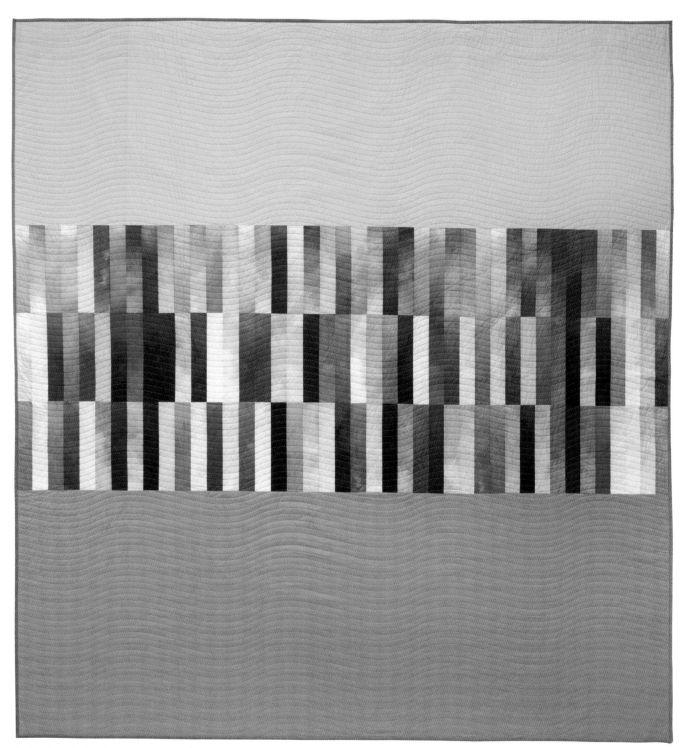

Quilted by Hello Stitch

MATERIALS

Ombré fabrics: 1 roll of 2½″-wide precut strips of your favorite collection, or cut your own strips.

Note ▶ *Most Roll-Ups come with 42 strips. If you use less, adjust the other requirements for the quilt to be a few inches narrower or add strips from another Roll-Up.*

Top-panel fabric: 2½ yards of Kona Cotton in Grellow or fabric of your choice

Bottom-panel fabric: 2½ yards of Kona Cotton in Yarrow or subtle woven yarn-dye

Note ▶ *I don't like seams in these large areas, so I used the entire length of yardage.*

Binding: ⅝ yard

Backing: 7¾ yards

Cotton batting: 93″ × 98″

DESIGNING THE QUILT

Arranging the Center Striped Panel

Start by arranging the center striped panel. On your table or design wall, organize the strips: Intermix the colors and flip the ombré from light to dark and dark to light, mixing and matching the colors that appeal to you. You can do it in a rainbow layout or make it more graphic, like blue to orange, yellow to gray, or pink to teal. More pop and drama will come to your layout when you add super darks next to super lights. Once you're happy with the strips, audition the fabrics for the top and bottom fields of the quilt to determine the large areas of color you desire.

CUTTING

Cutting is based on 42″ usable width of fabric (WOF).

Top-panel fabric

• Cut 1 piece 84″ × 26″ from Grellow.

Bottom-panel fabric

• Cut 1 piece 84″ × 31″ from Yarrow.

CONSTRUCTION

Sewing the Strips Together

1. With right sides together, stitch the 2 center strips together along the long edges from left to right.

2. Add the next strip, sewing from right to left. Continue adding strips for 10 total. Press the seams in one direction.

Note ▶ *Sewing the strips together in alternating directions helps prevent the section from being skewed.*

3. Repeat Steps 1 and 2 to make 2 more sections of 10 strips and 1 section of 12 strips.

4. Sew all 4 sections together. Press the seams in one direction.

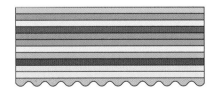

Trimming and Assembling the Center Panel

1. Lay out the sewn strip set. Using a removable chalk or fabric marker, divide the panel into 3 sections 11½″ × the length of the panel (84″ approximately) and decide what leftover you are going to cut off. 3 sections of 11½″ leaves about 6″– 8″ of unused parts. Trim into 3 sections along the drawn lines.

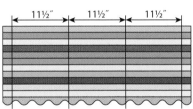
11½″   11½″   11½″

TIP The leftover pieces can be used on the backing or in another scrap-style quilt.

2. Arrange the sections as shown, turning the center section to be opposite of the outer sections.

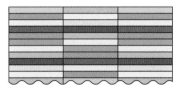

3. Sew an outside section to each side of the center section, matching up each seam by nesting the seams as you go. Press the seams open.

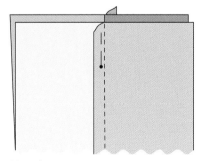

Nested seams

Adding the Top and Bottom Panels

1. Position the center panel and top panel with right sides together and pin.

2. Sew together. Press the seam away from the center panel.

3. Repeat Steps 1 and 2 to add the bottom panel.

Finishing

Layer, baste, quilt, and bind using your favorite method.

Hearth Quilt

Finished quilt: 68½″ × 89½″

Hearth is my riff on the traditional House block made jumbo and modern. The central eight-pointed star is hand appliquéd and is a symbol of hope, joy, and goodness. The hues are inspired by the colorful life we live under our roof, while the silent clouds move above our heads, reflecting the beauty of light and time.

Pieced with assistance from Kristen Takakuwa; quilted by Hello Stitch and Jennifer Sampou

Photo by Todd Hensley

MATERIALS

Full-range ombré fabrics work best with this large-scale pattern (see Full-Range Ombrés, page 12).

Choose colors for your house that remind you of the special beings who live with you. Celebrating the full width of selvage-to-selvage ombrés, this is an easy project with few seams. You might want to stitch family names in this piece to make it more personal. Don't forget to put a label on the back (or front!) for posterity.

Sky: 1⅛ yards

Ocean: ⅝ yard

Evening: ⅞ yard

Fog, Storm, and Spa: ¾ yard each

Dawn: 1¼ yards

Sunset: 1¾ yards

Blush, Ember, and Sunburst: ¾ yard each

Binding: ⅝ yard

Backing: 5½ yards

Batting: 77″ × 98″

Double-stick fusible web (like Steam-A-Seam 2): ½ yard

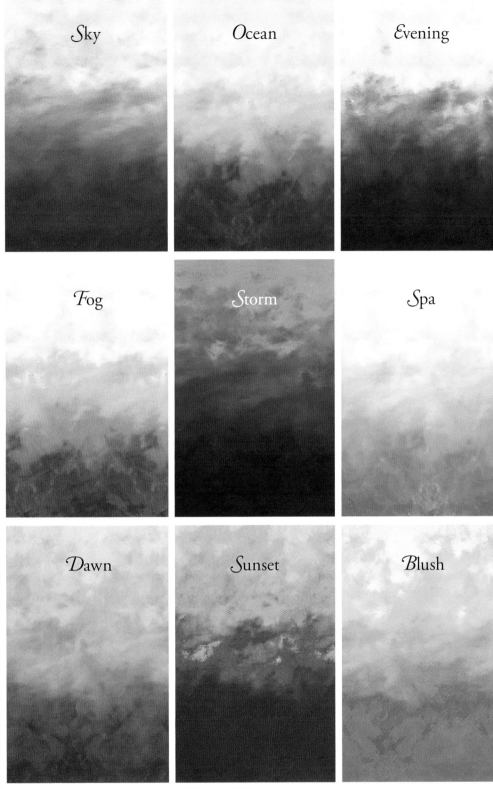

Sky   Ocean   Evening

Fog   Storm   Spa

Dawn   Sunset   Blush

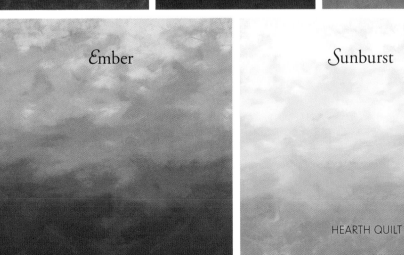

Ember   Sunburst

DESIGNING THE QUILT

What color is your nest? Choose a palette that reflects a feeling you wish to enhance. Do you want a soft, sun-washed mood or vibrant brights? Is green your vibe, or do you prefer rich neutrals? I encourage you to process a few different palettes, mixing and playing with color. Then settle on a combination that sings to you. It helps to invest in larger cuts to get an accurate feel of the colors you are choosing—a half yard should do the trick.

Finalize your palette; then double-check the fabric values and colors to make sure the star contrasts with the background house and rooftop as well as the base of the house. See how the top point of the star is a light value with pinkish hues and looks great against the dark navy and gray of the rooftop? The darker points pop off the lighter areas of the roof. Study each star point and center. I fussy cut these big diamond shapes and cut more than I needed to have options.

Notice how the blue star tips pop off the warm hues of house?

Photo by Jennifer Sampou

CUTTING

Cutting is based on 42″ useable width of fabric (WOF).

Rooftop / sky / house base

- Cut 1 strip 9″ × WOF each of Sky and Evening.

- Cut 2 strips 9″ × WOF each of Fog, Storm, Spa, Blush, Ember, and Sunburst.

- Cut 4 strips 9″ × WOF of Dawn.

- Cut 6 strips 9″ × WOF of Sunset.

Eight-pointed star

- Cut 1 strip 9½″ × WOF each of Ocean and Evening; subcut 2 diamonds each.

- Cut 2 strips 9½″ × WOF of Sky; subcut 4 diamonds from light and dark areas with the most interest.

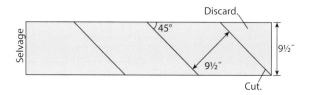

CONSTRUCTION

Making the Rooftop and Sky

1. Arrange one strip each of Sky, Spa, Fog, and Storm for the left side, as shown. Note that the ombré flips from dark to light and light to dark.

2. You have strips longer than you need. Choose the part of the ombré you like best and trim the strips to 35¼″ long. There is no set way; select whatever you like. Sew the 4 strips together in order: Sky to Spa to Fog to Storm. Press the seams open.

3. Arrange one strip each of Fog, Evening, Spa, and Storm for the right side, as shown. Note that the ombré flips from dark to light and light to dark. Choose the part of the ombré you like best and trim the strips to 35¼″ long. Sew the 4 strips together in order: Fog to Evening to Spa to Storm. Press the seams open.

4. This yields 2 large rectangle units 34½″ × 35¼″, one for the left side and one for the right side.

5. Measure ⅜″ up from the bottom left corner and mark on the edge. Measure ⅜″ down from the top right corner and mark on the edge. Connect these marks and cut the left rooftop square diagonally from bottom left to top right.

6. Cut the right rooftop unit diagonally in the same manner, except measuring ⅜″ down from the top left corner and ⅜″ up from the bottom right corner.

Left side of sky/roof

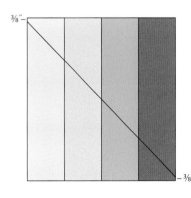

Right side of sky/roof

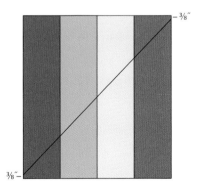

Note ▶ Important! Read Steps 5 and 6 twice and cut once. *This is very important! If you cut in the wrong direction, you will not get the correct angle you need when creating the sky to roof shape.*

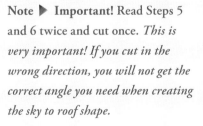

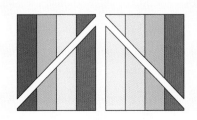

7. Place the upper half of the left rooftop unit right sides together to the lower half of the right rooftop unit. Match the seams and sew together. Press the seam open.

8. Match the remaining pieces in the same manner and sew together. Press the seam open.

9. Sew the 2 units together down the center seam to create the rooftop.

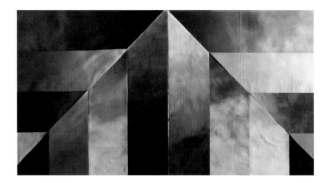

Making the House Base

1. With right sides together, match the darkest ends of each pair of 9″ × WOF strips of Sunburst, Blush, and Ember. Sew each pair together and press the seams open.

2. Sew 2 sets each of Sunset and Dawn in the same manner, matching the darkest ends. Press the seams open.

3. The last strip is also Sunset. This time, match the lightest ends with right sides together and press the seam open.

4. For each of the 8 pieced strips, measure 15″ from the seam and trim. Then measure 40½″ on the other side of the seam and trim. Finished strip measures 55½″.

5. Arrange the 8 strips in order from left to right: Dawn, Sunset (dark bottom), Blush, Sunset (light bottom), Sunset (dark bottom), Ember, Sunburst, and Dawn. Sew all 8 strips together, matching the seams, to make the house base. Press the seams open.

6. With right sides together, match up the seams and sew the rooftop/sky unit to the house base. Press the seam open.

15″ extended strips at bottom with fabric names labeled

Photo by Jennifer Sampou

Arranging the Eight-Pointed Star

Play with the placement of the diamonds on top of the rooftop / sky / house base. Take photos of various layouts and audition different sets of diamonds with the few extra you cut out. Alternate light and dark diamonds to accentuate center points. Dark outer points look better on medium and light fabric ground and light points look better on medium to dark grounds. If you are not pleased with final layout, cut out a few more diamonds to get the arrangement you like.

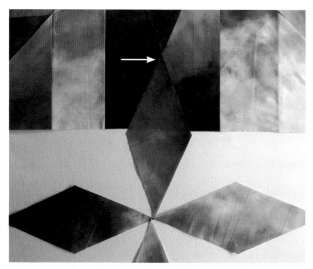

Poor contrast between star points and background needs improvement

Photo by Jennifer Sampou

1. With right sides together, sew 2 diamonds together. Repeat to make 4 pairs. Press all the seams in the same direction.

2. Sew the pairs into halves and press the seams in same direction as before.

3. Sew the halves together to create the star. Press all the seams in the same direction, carefully pressing the center point so it lies flat.

Appliquéing the Star to the House

1. Place the star on the house, lining up the top and bottom points to the center seams. Line up the inner angles at 1 and 11 o'clock, just covering the horizontal seam where the house meets the roof.

2. Using double-stick fusible web or your favorite way to adhere an appliqué to the background, secure the star motif in place. I chose to appliqué the star in place by hand using needle-turn appliqué. You could also use a machine satin stitch or raw-edge appliqué.

Finishing

Layer, baste, quilt, and bind using your favorite method. I chose to add some big hand stitches around the star, which adds nice texture.

Sunset Lake Quilt

Finished quilt: 88″ × 105½″

The sun dropping below a lake makes its way through the atmosphere, changing every moment. The bold horizon line where the evening sky meets the cool, placid water is set off by hot colors with flashes of bright light. Small squares on point sparkle like jewels. Sewing large pieces of ombré fabric using my Jumbo Octagon Shimmer Templates (available at jennifersampou.com) is a perfect way to sew the pieces together accurately.

Pieced with assistance from Kristen Takakuwa and Ashleigh Pevey, quilted by Jess Zeigler

Prairie Sky	Storm	Noble Purple	Midnight
Celestial	Nightfall	Cerise	Sundance
Heather	Haze	Cloud	Atmosphere
Blush	Mist	Evening	Sunset

Kona Cotton in Meringue

Essex Yarn Dyed Metallic in Opal

Essex Yarn Dyed Metallic in Crystal

MATERIALS

When you choose ombrés, you will find the nuances from one inch to another are what make them so luscious. These sixteen fabrics range greatly in color and value. I increased the fabric requirements a bit so you have extra fabric to play with. It's important to know that leftover blocks are part of the process.

TIP

For dramatic results like those pictured, choose full-range ombrés so you can achieve a variety of saturated darks to the palest of blue sky at the top (see Full-Range Ombrés, page 12).

Prairie Sky, Storm, Noble Purple, Midnight, Celestial, Nightfall, Cerise, Sundance, and Heather: ½ yard each

Haze, Cloud, Atmosphere, Blush, and Mist: 1 yard each

Evening and Sunset: 1½ yards each

Kona Cotton in Meringue: 1 fat quarter

Essex Yarn Dyed Metallic in Opal and Crystal: ¾ yard each

Binding: ¾ yard

Backing: 8 yards

Batting: 96″ × 114″

TIP

At the time of publishing, fifteen of these colors are sold in a Sunset bundle of ½-yard precuts. So you could buy 2 bundles plus an extra ½ yard of Evening, Sunset, and Prairie Sky. You would still need the yardage above of the Kona Cotton and Essex Yarn Dyed Metallic fabrics.

VALUE STUDY

This quilt will challenge and hone your skills to gain a deeper understanding of value. To begin digesting how you will make this happen, I break down the ombré fabrics into seven broad sections of value: pale, light, medium light, medium, medium dark, dark and very dark. Within these basic sections are deeper breakdowns.

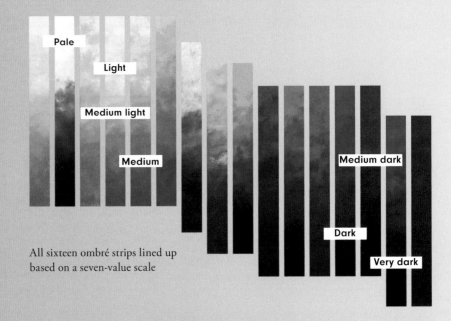

All sixteen ombré strips lined up based on a seven-value scale

Fabric to fabric, the value of these ombrés vary from light to dark, more dramatic to less dramatic. There is no perfect formula, so you have an extremely broad range of color and value and not straightforward instructions that say, "Cut every fabric this one way."

When you begin to mix and match, you will learn more about the relativity of value. These value sections give you a foundation for the placement of the fabric.

Below is an example of how much variety of value is found in just Celestial, which is a medium dark to very dark ombré. See how we get eight shades of kites in that one fabric?

Eight shades of kites from Celestial

Photo by Jennifer Sampou

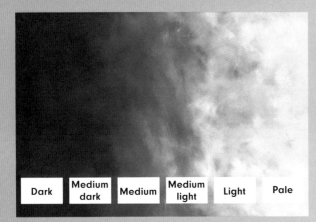

Sky separated into six sections in one single fabric

To digest the big picture of value again, look at this photo in black and white or gray scale. It clearly illustrates the full range of value from inky black to the palest of blues.

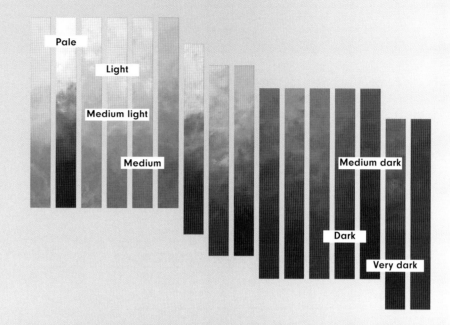

Pale

Light

Medium light

Medium

Medium dark

Dark

Very dark

Also note that what may seem like a light fabric when put against a dark ombré can also be a dark fabric when put next to pale ones. Color is relative when it comes to value. You have to do this yourself to believe it! Look at these examples. They appear to be different-colored squares, but it's the same color!

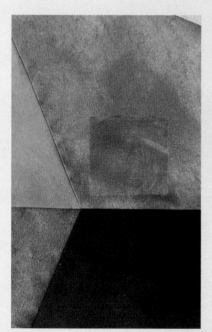
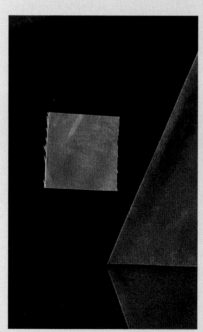
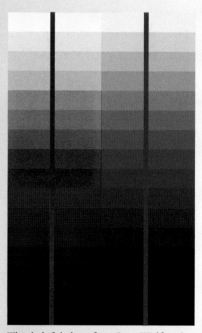

Hard to believe, but the little blue square shown above is the same piece of fabric. It looks different when placed on a light versus a dark background.

Photos by Jennifer Sampou

This helpful chart from Joen Wolfrom's *Color Play, Second Edition* provides a telling graphic of value at play. The center stripe is a solid color. Her book is a must for quilters.

You may need to read this more than once. Cut your fabrics, play with the shapes, and then read it again.

Open your fabrics and lay out all 19 pieces. Organize the fabrics from darks to lights so you can see everything you have. Studying your fabrics and moving them around will be an invaluable step when it comes to knowing what to cut where.

As you begin to design from the bottom up, super-saturated and very dark lake colors gradually give way to pale heavens, with a burst of hot warmth midway that bounces and reflects pinks above and burgundies in the water below.

These images below show the variety of value and color used in this quilt.

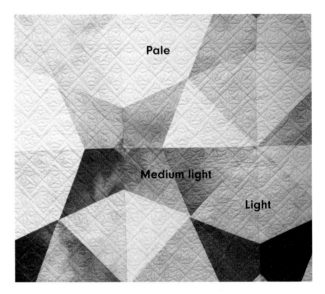

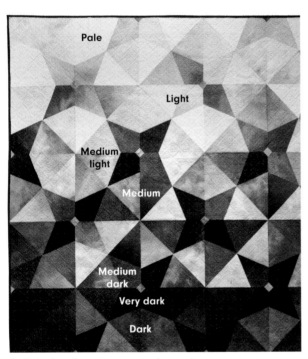

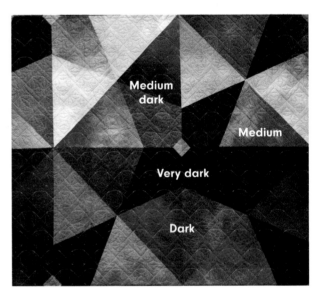

Quilt broken down into seven value sections

Notice above that there are areas of pale. For instance, every fabric isn't that value, yet the overall feeling is. A darker value in this section adds interest and energy to your piece. Another example is the light peach, set immediately above the water's edge, which creates a sparkle in the dark area. Remember: These tips are the secret to making a good quilt *great*. Just like the artist who brushes a few accent strokes to bring life to their painting.

CUTTING

Cutting is based on 42" usable width of fabric (WOF). Use the Sunset Lake patterns (pages 43–45) for cutting the kites and triangles. Join the halves of the patterns on the join lines as you trace the full shapes onto template plastic.

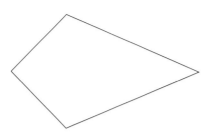

Template cutting for kites

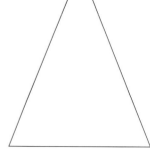

Template cutting for triangles

Or you can order custom Jumbo Octagon Shimmer Templates from jennifersampou.com.

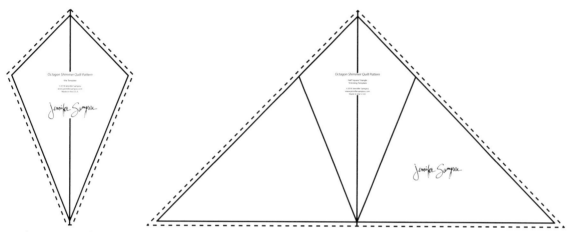

Jumbo Octagon Shimmer Templates

Do not cut all your pieces in the beginning. Cut about 75 percent of what you will need, keeping leftover fabric intact to use later for the kites and triangles. I suggest you cut a good variety with about 10 extra pieces of each shape so that you can play with the layout.

There are 120 triangles and 60 kites in this quilt. Each ½ yard yields about 4–6 triangles and 3–5 kites. Build this top consciously and mindfully. Once you have most of the blocks laid out, go back to your materials and finish fussy cutting the colors you need in the kite and triangle areas.

There are various ways to get kites and triangles cut from each ½-yard piece.

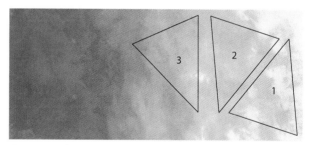

Cut 3 triangles in lightest area of Blush with extra for later decision.

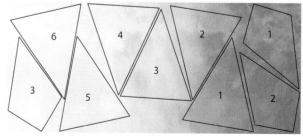

Cut 3 kites in darkest and lightest area of Atmosphere, with 6 triangles in middle.

Note ▶ *Begin with the kites and the darkest ombrés. This establishes the dark kites first, and you build the triangles onto the kites, one Half-Square Triangle block at a time. Create the quilt from the bottom up.*

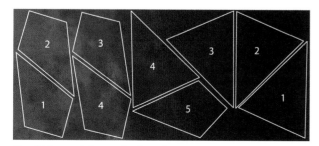

Cut 5 kites and 4 triangles from Cerise.

Kites

Fussy cut:

- 20–30 kites, 2 to 3 per fabric from the very dark areas of 11 of the darkest ombrés—blues, dark grays, purples, and blacks (Prairie Sky, Storm, Noble Purple, Midnight, Celestial, Nightfall, Heather, Haze, and Evening)

- 5–8 kites, 1 per fabric from the dark parts of ombrés—burgundies, purples, and grays (Prairie Sky, Storm, Noble Purple, Midnight, Celestial, Nightfall, Cerise, Sundance, and Haze)

- 5–8 kites, 1 per fabric from the medium-dark parts of ombrés—pinks, reds, purples, and grays (Prairie Sky, Storm, Noble Purple, Celestial, Nightfall, Cerise, Sundance, Heather, Haze, and Cloud)

- 7–10 kites, 1 to 2 per fabric from the medium parts of ombrés—pinks, reds, blues, purples, and grays (Storm, Cerise, Sundance, Heather, Haze, Cloud, Atmosphere, Blush, Mist, Evening, and Sunset)

- 3–6 kites, 1 to 2 per fabric from the medium-light parts of ombrés—blues, purples, and grays (Heather, Cloud, Atmosphere, and Mist)

- 5–8 kites, 1 to 2 per fabric from the light parts of ombrés—pinks, blues, and purples (Heather, Atmosphere, Blush, Mist, and Evening)

Note ▶ *A total of 70 kites can be potentially cut now, but don't feel like you have to cut them all at once. I didn't! Begin with 45–50, knowing that the last 20–25 kites will be decided and cut later.*

Triangles

I cut the triangles larger than the template. Then I used my octagon triangle-trimming method to ensure exact piecing. Watch my video tutorial about using the templates; for the link, see Bonus Videos (page 71).

Fussy cut:

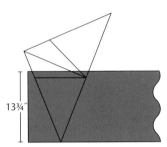

13¾"

Optional cutting and trimming method (Jumbo Octagon Shimmer Templates)

- 5–7 triangles, 1 to 2 from the very dark areas of the darkest ombrés—charcoals, purples, and navies (Prairie Sky, Storm, Noble Purple, Midnight, Celestial, Nightfall, Heather, Haze, and Evening)

- 27–40 triangles, 3 to 4 per fabric from the dark parts of ombrés—burgundies, purples, blues, and grays (Prairie Sky, Storm, Noble Purple, Midnight, Celestial, Nightfall, Cerise, Sundance, Haze, Cloud, Evening, and Sunset)

- 7–10 triangles, 1 per fabric from the medium-dark parts of ombrés—pinks, reds, purples, and grays (Prairie Sky, Storm, Noble Purple, Midnight, Celestial, Nightfall, Cerise, Sundance, Haze, Cloud, Evening, and Sunset)

- 14–20 triangles, 1 to 2 per fabric from the medium parts of ombrés—pinks, reds, blues, purples, and grays (Storm, Cerise, Sundance, Heather, Haze, Cloud, Atmosphere, Blush, Mist, Evening, and Sunset)

- 10–14 triangles, 1 to 2 per fabric from the medium-light parts of ombrés—pinks, oranges, blues, purples, and grays (Nightfall, Heather, Haze, Cloud, Atmosphere, Blush, Mist, Evening, and Sunset)

- 16–23 triangles, 2 to 3 per fabric from the light parts of ombrés—pinks, yellows, blues, purples, and grays (Nightfall, Heather, Haze, Cloud, Atmosphere, Blush, Mist, and Evening)

- 11–16 triangles, 2 per fabric from solids and the palest parts of ombrés—pinks, yellows, blues, purples, and grays (Kona Cotton in Meringue, Essex Yarn Dyed Metallic in Opal, Essex Yarn Dyed Metallic in Crystal, Heather, Haze, Atmosphere, Blush, Mist, and Evening)

Note ▶ *A total of 130 triangles can be potentially cut now, but don't cut them all at once. I didn't! Begin with 90–100, knowing that the last 30–40 triangles will be decided and cut later.*

Small squares

- Cut strips of medium to light colors of leftovers 1¾″ × whatever length you can get. Subcut 15 sets of 4 matching squares 1¾″ × 1¾″ in oranges, blues, teals, purples, and lavenders. Keep the squares in sets of 4 since they create the 4 tips of the right angles that are pieced together later to form the centers of the big stars.

CONSTRUCTION

1. Lay out all your pieces on the floor or design wall (They won't fit on your table most likely!). Decide how you like your half-square triangles arranged.

TIP I found it helpful to label each half-square triangle 1–60. Be sure to take photos with your smartphone.

2. Sew a lighter-colored triangle to each side of a darker-colored kite to create a large half-square triangle. Press the seams open.

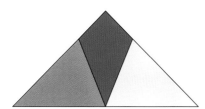

3. Continue to make half-square triangles, grouping them in sets of 4, working from very dark half-square triangles of the lake to the palest sky at the top.

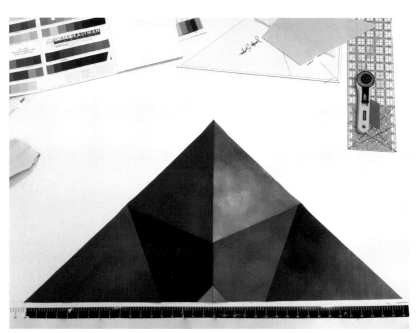

Photo by Jennifer Sampou

Note ▶ *If you choose the octagon triangle-trimming method of cutting, center the oversized triangle on the kite's edge and sew. After the seams are pressed open, trim the half-square triangle to size using the Jumbo Octagon Shimmer triangle ruler. Match the seams to the printed kite lines on the ruler. This will give you more accurate blocks to work with.*

4. Once you have decided on the placement of the first group of cut pieces, cut and piece all 60 half-square triangles.

TIP It's a good idea to take a photo in black and white to evaluate your darks and lights and to move anything before sewing the colorful small squares to the kite tips.

5. To add the small square highlights for each Star block, draw a line from corner to corner on the wrong side of each square with a chalk or light pencil. Line up to the kite tip, right sides together, and pin. Sew on the drawn line. Flip, press, and trim off the dog-ear, leaving a ¼″ seam allowance.

Wrong side

Right side

6. The quilt is pieced on a diagonal. Sew 4 half-square triangles together to create a large Star block.

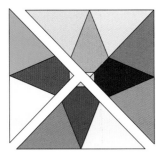

Right side of star

7. Repeat Step 6 to make 10 large Star blocks, and pair sets of half-square triangles to make 9 Half-Star blocks.

Final Setting

1. Arrange your 19 blocks and 2 remaining half-square triangles from darks to lights to get the ombré effect across the quilt.

2. Sew the blocks into diagonal rows. Press the seams open.

3. Sew the rows together. Press the seams open.

Finishing

Layer, baste, quilt, and bind using your favorite method.

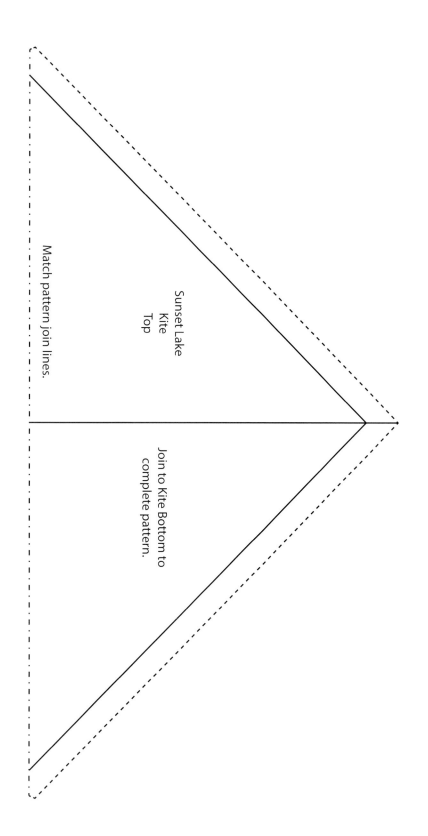

Sunset Lake
Kite
Top

Match pattern join lines.

Join to Kite Bottom to
complete pattern.

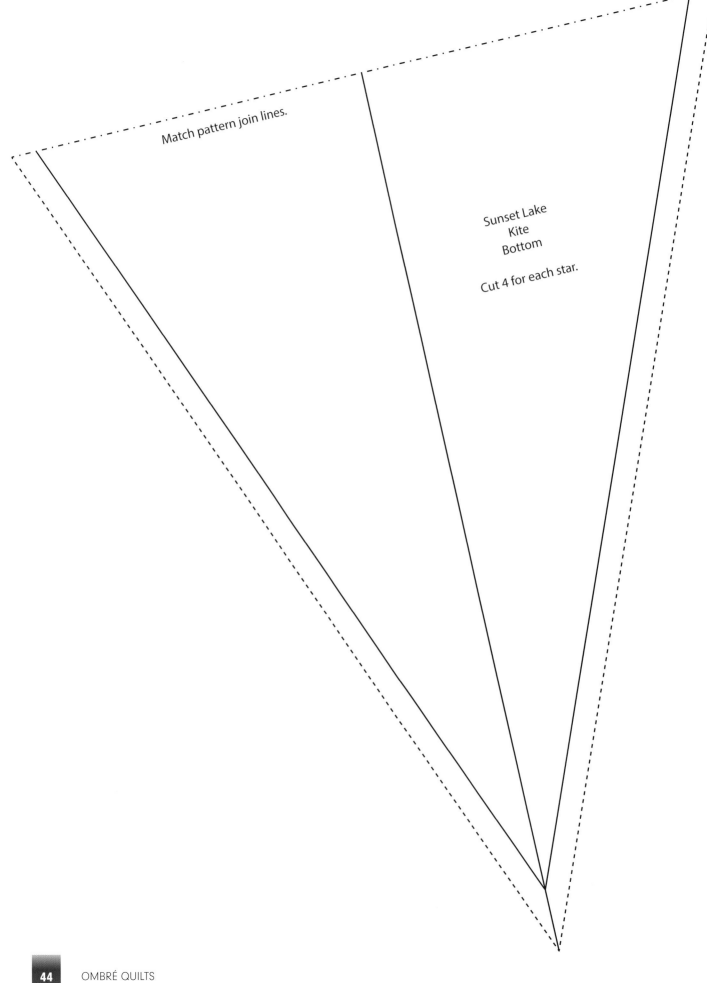

Match pattern join lines.

Sunset Lake
Kite
Bottom

Cut 4 for each star.

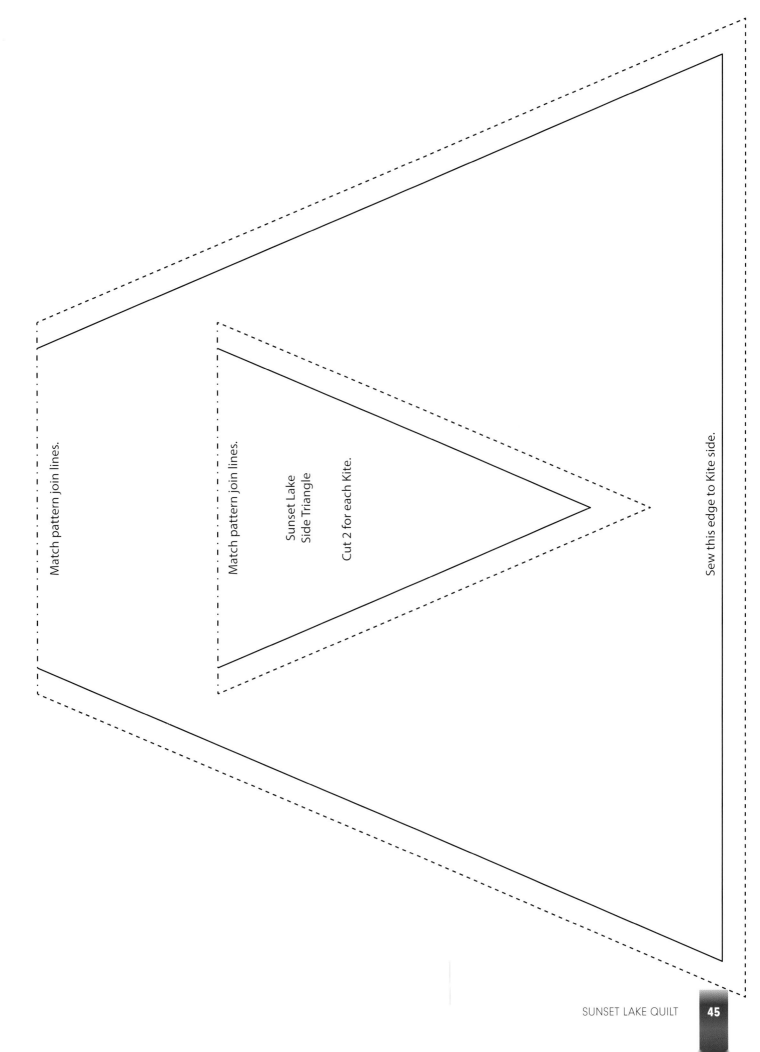

Match pattern join lines.

Match pattern join lines.

Sunset Lake
Side Triangle

Cut 2 for each Kite.

Sew this edge to Kite side.

Whale and *I* Quilt **Finished quilt:** 53″ × 59″

Whale and I comes straight from my heart. My love for our natural planet and compassion for all its beings is how I am hardwired. Part of the book proceeds will be donated to California Whale Rescue.

Quilted by Jenny Lyon

I've also provided design options if you prefer mermaids or divers. The whale can be placed in all angles for a different layout or reduced 50 percent to make a baby to go with the adult; a mermaid can be deeper underwater or flipped, or you could add two divers. There are lots of possibilities.

MATERIALS

Yardage is based on 42″-wide WOF.

Scraps for whale and human

Assorted fabrics: 30–40 pieces at least 8″ × 14″ each *or* 20 quarter-yard pieces of ombré fabrics to be used repeatedly, cutting light and dark areas within each piece (I used Cerise, Sunset, Dawn, Atmosphere, Cloud, Sunburst, Sea Glass, Ember, Powder, Blush, and Kona Cotton in Butter, Wasabi, Pickle, and Persimmon. Be sure to use a variety of super dark to very light ombré fabrics for your whale and human.)

Photo by Jennifer Sampou

| Cerise | Sunset | Dawn | Atmosphere | Cloud | Sunburst | Sea Glass | Ember |

| Powder | Blush | Spa | Azure | Kona Cotton in Butter | Kona Cotton in Wasabi | Kona Cotton in Pickle | Kona Cotton in Persimmon |

Sky and sea for background

Spa: 1½ yards for sky

Azure: 1½ yards for sea

Other materials

Binding: ½ yard

Backing: 3½ yards

Batting: 61″ × 67″

Foundation paper (I like the Carol Doak's Foundation Paper by C&T Publishing.)

Double-stick fusible web (like Lite Steam-A-Seam 2): ½ yard

Stabilizing paper for machine appliqué (I used Wash-Away Appliqué Sheets by C&T Publishing.)

School glue stick

Brayer or wooden roller (It's nice to have by the machine if you'd rather roll than press.)

Add-A-Quarter ruler (available from cmdesignsonline.com)

Background fabrics on design wall

Photo by Jennifer Sampou

DESIGNING THE QUILT

Choose your sky and sea colors first. Before you cut up your colorful scraps, lay them on the sky and sea background and take out any that are too close in color or value to the background. For example, originally I picked light blue for the body of the whale, but it was too close to the Azure sea background and didn't pop enough. I swapped out a deeper purple from the tail tip and put blue there instead.

The deeper purple worked great against the Spa sky. Remember that color and value is all relative; what may seem dark and rich or light and bright depends on what other color or values you are putting it next to.

Whale and Human

Arrange the fabrics.

The whale is a huge animal; it deserves big, bold colors for its back and light colors for its belly. The front and back whale fins are in bright colors to give the illusion that sunlight is hitting the fins and that they are coming out of the body. They also pop against the darker water and the belly of the whale. Paying close attention hones your color and value skills. Take a few rounds of playing with fabrics to get it right.

For the human, use lighter colors. I like blocking similar color families together without doing a rainbow effect. Also note that I have used similar colors in the human as in the whale—just lighter values of some.

The extremities (last outer fabric piece) of both subjects must also be thought through and tested. The tip of the hands, toes, head, tail, nose, and fins should be carefully evaluated against the background color. Be sure that there's good contrast so the subject doesn't look unfinished or cut off.

CUTTING

Cutting is based on 42" useable width of fabric (WOF).

Sky and sea

- Cut a 53½" × 20" rectangle of Spa for the sky. I cut 1" off the selvage of the lighter side so the sky is contrasted properly against the sea. You can play with folding the fabric at different areas to get the look you want for the sea-to-sky relationship.

- Cut a 53½" × 40" rectangle of Azure for the sea. I cut about 4" off the darkest selvage to use for paper piecing the whale. The nice thing about this ombré background is that it is so easy to use and showcases the beautiful gradation of the full ombré. The selvages are the bottom and top of the sea.

Human and whale

- I start by cutting pieces at least double in size. I don't worry about the waste—I would rather cut off the excess than have to rip out with a seam ripper or add an additional seam and fabric extension.

CONSTRUCTION

Sea and Sky

Sew the sky to the sea. Press the seam open. The piece should measure 53½" × 59½"; trim if needed.

Paper Piecing the Whale and Human

Patterns are reversed for paper piecing. Seam allowances are ¼".

Paper piecing tricks you, especially when the seams are angled and you are looking at the back side of the pattern.

Note ▶ *My favorite paper-piecing book is* Adventures in Paper Piecing & Design *by Sarah Elizabeth Sharp. It has excellent detail and provides opportunity for deeper learning.*

 TIP

Don't rush. Paper piecing usually begins with a few head scratches, a trip to the fridge to see what's to eat ... and then returning with a few more head scratches. Take the time to read the instructions carefully.

PAPER PIECING THE HUMAN

Use the Whale and I *patterns (pages 54–63) to make the foundations for the various appliqué shapes and sections.*

Choose the human, the diver with fins, or the mermaid. Remember that the pattern piece is printed to show the back side because that is how paper piecing is done. You work on the mirror image of the subject because when you are done sewing and trimming, you turn it over and it shows the clean finished piece. Ta-da! When cutting the fabrics, remember that the piece is being placed on unprinted side of pattern and that the wrong sides go together. Hold the fabric up to the pattern and check to make sure the piece will cover its pattern area with at least ¼″ over the stitch line.

1. Photocopy the pattern onto foundation paper.

2. Roughly cut around the human shape to remove the excess paper, but don't cut into the armpit, between the legs, or into the neck.

3. Flip the paper pattern over to the unmarked side. Starting with the top of the head, lightly glue or pin down the first fabric on the unprinted side, overlapping the solid line by about ¼″. Hold it up to light to check the placement.

4. With right sides together, align the second fabric strip with the first over the line between pieces 1 and 2. Pin or hold it in place.

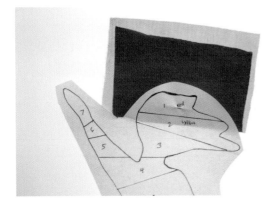

5. Flip the pattern over and sew on the solid line between pieces 1 and 2 through all 3 layers.

6. Press the second strip open with a brayer roller or a hot iron. I like both. It depends if it's cold in my studio— then I love a good hot iron.

7. Fold the pattern back on itself along the solid line between pieces 2 and 3. Trim the second strip to a ¼″ seam allowance using the Add-A-Quarter ruler.

8. Repeat Steps 4–7 to add the third strip in the same way. Continue this process, adding strips in numerical order to fill the entire pattern. Trim on the solid line.

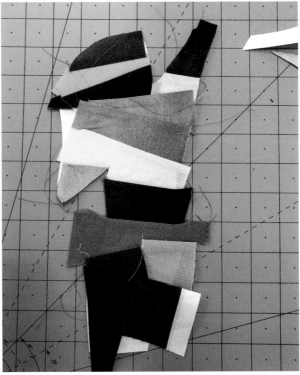

Photo by Jennifer Sampou

TIPS

- I like pre-folding my paper pieces to establish the stitching line before I begin. It helps to speed up the process and increases accuracy.

- Shorten the stitch length on your machine (1.2 on a BERNINA), which will make the paper tear off more easily when you remove it later.

- Watch my video tutorials about paper piecing; for the links, see Bonus Videos (page 71).

PAPER PIECING THE WHALE

The whale is made up of 9 paper-pieced units: nose, head, throat, front fin, back fin, mid-body, rump, tail, and tail tips. Seam allowances have been added to the pattern where needed so the units can be sewn together after paper piecing. For each section, follow Paper Piecing the Human, Steps 1–8 (previous page).

Nose A

1. It's important to pick a contrasting fabric since this is the beginning of the whale. I even had it relate to the human's outstretched arm to form a color connection with Kona Cotton in Pickle, Wasabi, and Glacier.

2. Trim the nose on the outer line.

TIP If you are not going to finish the project quickly, leave ½" or so to trim later, when you are ready to finish. This prevents frayed edges.

Head B and Throat C

1. The color of B3 is the same as the nose A1.

2. Trim off the excess on the B1–3 unit to start on B4.

3. Work down the head like in Paper Piecing the Human until you end at B10.

4. Piece C, starting with the C1 in the middle of the throat area.

Note ▶ *Matching seams exactly can be tricky and takes precision in paper piecing. So let's keep those matched seams to a minimum! That is why I designed the belly of the whale to have the striated gray-and-white pattern that is **not** matched unit to unit! Have fun and don't sweat the small stuff … at least in this part. You only have to match where the colored back meets the white belly.*

Front Fin D

To get the fin to appear like it's coming out of the body, make F2 and D6 darker than D5. Make the fin colors bright and be sure to choose a color that won't blend in with sea fabric for D2 and D3.

Back Fin E

Note that the color is punched up against the dark sea color.

Mid-Body F

F2 is same color as D6.

Rump G, Tail H, and Tail Tips I

To make the tail look like it's out of the water, H3 and I1 should be color related, I1 being a lighter value and similar color family to H3. This creates a transparency effect.

Assembling the Whale

1. Start by sewing Nose A to Head B. Press the seam open.

2. With right sides together, pin Head B to Throat C, matching the seams at B4 and C8. Pin directly through the pressed-open seam at B4 to the seam at C8. Then pin on each side to stabilize and keep it from slipping to match this one point of B and C.

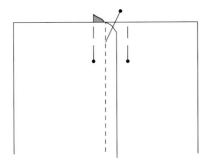

Pin seams.

> **TIP**
> I chose to fold the foundation paper back before sewing the seams together to reduce bulk. Therefore, I sewed along the edge of the folded-back paper, not catching it in the seam allowance.

3. Sew together Front Fin D to Mid-Body F. Press the seams open.

4. Sew together Rump G to Tail H to Tail Tips I. Press the seams open.

5. Sew ABC to DF. Press the seam open.

6. Sew at the notches on Back Fin E.

7. Sew ABCDFE to GHI. Be sure to match the seam at F3 to the seam at G7. Press the seams open.

8. Trim away any dog-ears, overlaps, or excess, leaving ¼" of the fabric outside the edge line.

The good news is you're done paper piecing! But don't clean up the edges yet.

ADDING THE APPLIQUÉS

Watch my video tutorial about machine appliqué; for the link, see Bonus Videos (page 71).

1. Gently remove the paper from the whale and human. Be careful not to pull at the seams.

2. Cut a piece of double-stick fusible web to extend ½″ beyond the entire human body. Iron the body to the fusible web per the manufacturer's directions. Remove the paper and trim off the excess fusible web.

3. Cut 1″-wide pieces of double-stick fusible web to overlap the entire whale edge.

4. Press the fusible web on the back side of the whale and peel the paper off. Trim ¼″ off the edges.

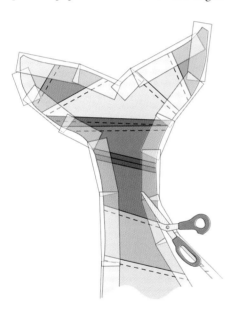

5. Position the whale with the whale tail seam at the sea-sky seam.

6. Place the human with the foot seam at the sea-sky seam.

7. Press stabilizing paper onto the back of the quilt top, behind the objects, to support appliquéing by machine.

8. Appliqué the whale and human to the background using a satin stitch with matching thread. It gives a clean finish and no pulling or wobbly edge when stabilized.

9. Tear away the excess stabilizer.

FINISHING

Layer, baste, quilt, and bind using your favorite method.

INVISIBLE BINDING

Here is how I made the invisible binding on *Whale and I*.

1. Cut 4 squares 4½″ × 4½″ from one end of the binding fabric.

2. Cut 6 strips 2½″ wide × the remaining width of the fabric.

3. Sew the 6 strips together and subcut 2 strips 49½″ and 2 strips 55½″.

4. Press the strips in half, wrong sides together.

5. Fold the 4½″ × 4½″ squares in half diagonally and press.

6. Pin the triangles to the front of the quilt at the corners, matching the raw edges.

7. Pin the 49½″ strips to the top and bottom of the quilt, starting 2″ from a corner, placing the strips over the triangles, and matching the raw edges.

8. Pin the 55½″ strips to the sides of the quilt in the same manner.

9. Stitch the binding to the quilt with a ¼″ seam.

10. Trim the corners and fold the binding to the back, gently poking the corners out. Press.

11. Hand stitch the binding to the back of the quilt.

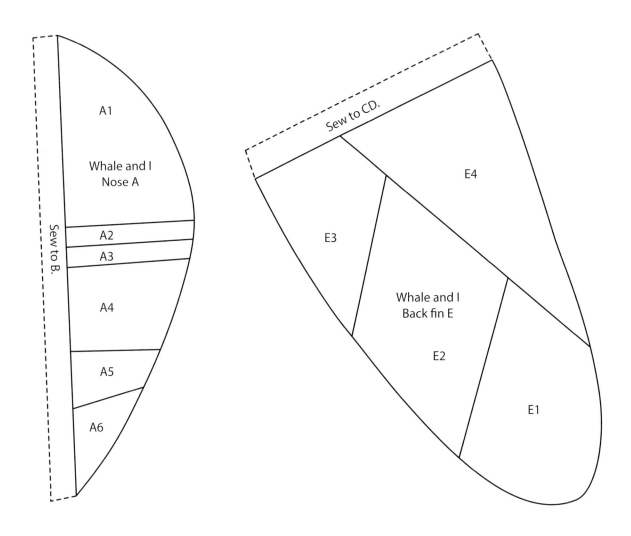

A1

Whale and I
Nose A

Sew to B.

A2

A3

A4

A5

A6

Sew to CD.

E4

E3

Whale and I
Back fin E

E2

E1

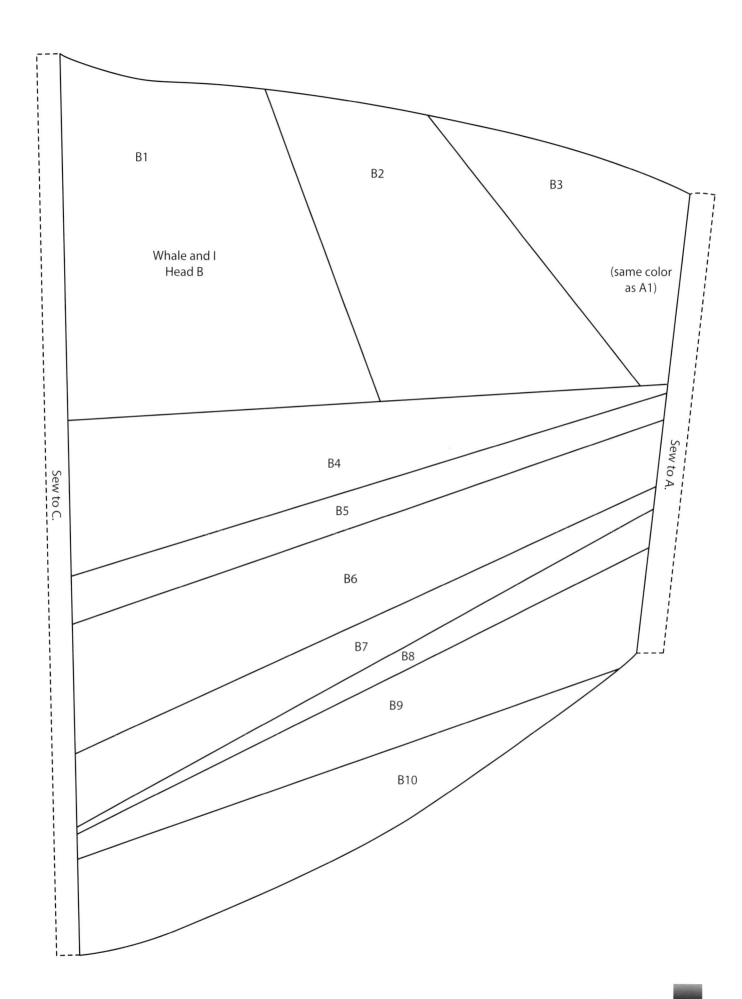

B1

Whale and I
Head B

B2

B3

(same color
as A1)

Sew to C.

Sew to A.

B4

B5

B6

B7

B8

B9

B10

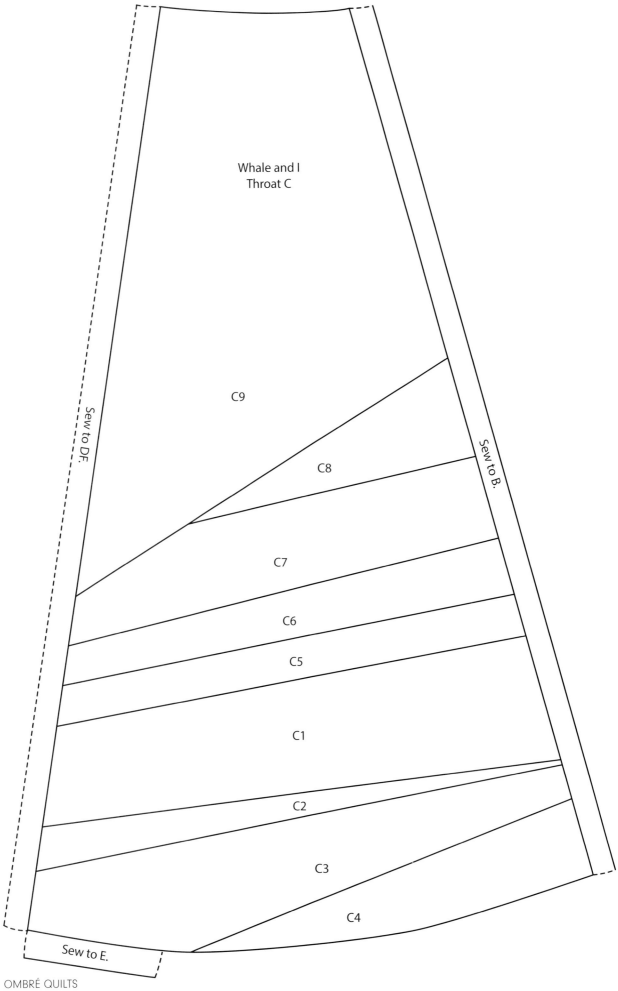

Whale and I
Throat C

Sew to DF.

Sew to B.

C9

C8

C7

C6

C5

C1

C2

C3

C4

Sew to E.

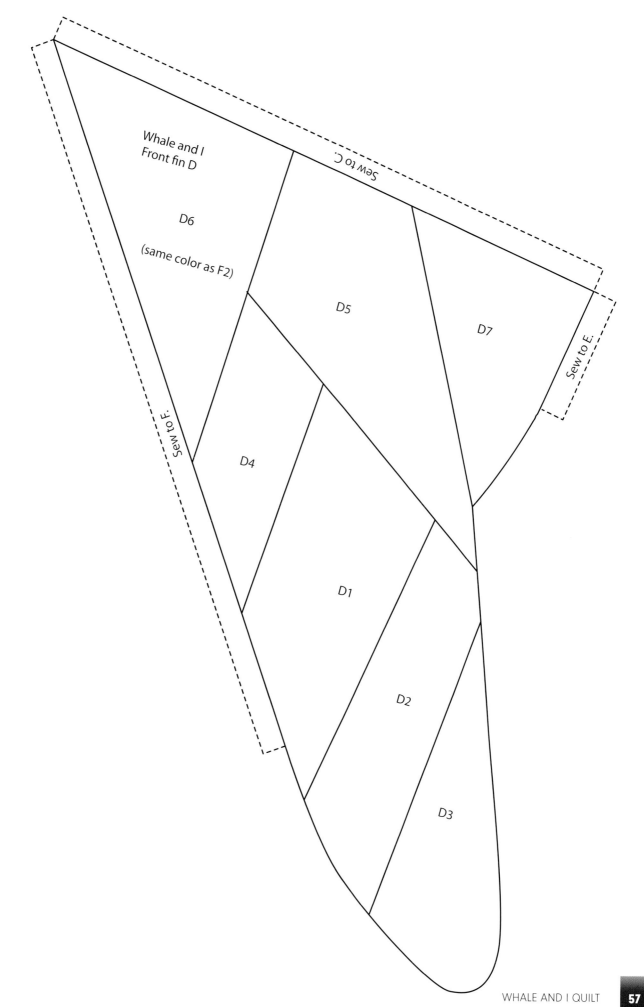

Whale and I
Front fin D

D6

(same color as F2)

D5

D7

D4

D1

D2

D3

Sew to C.

Sew to E.

Sew to F.

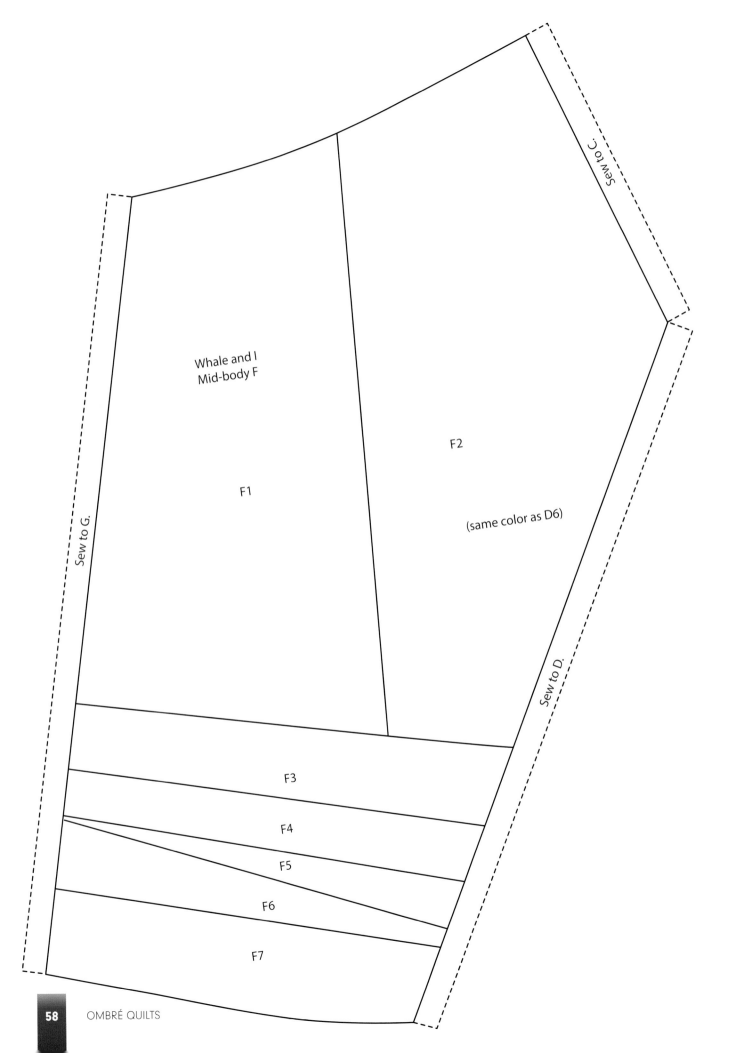

Sew to C.

Sew to G.

Sew to D.

Whale and I
Mid-body F

F2

(same color as D6)

F1

F3

F4

F5

F6

F7

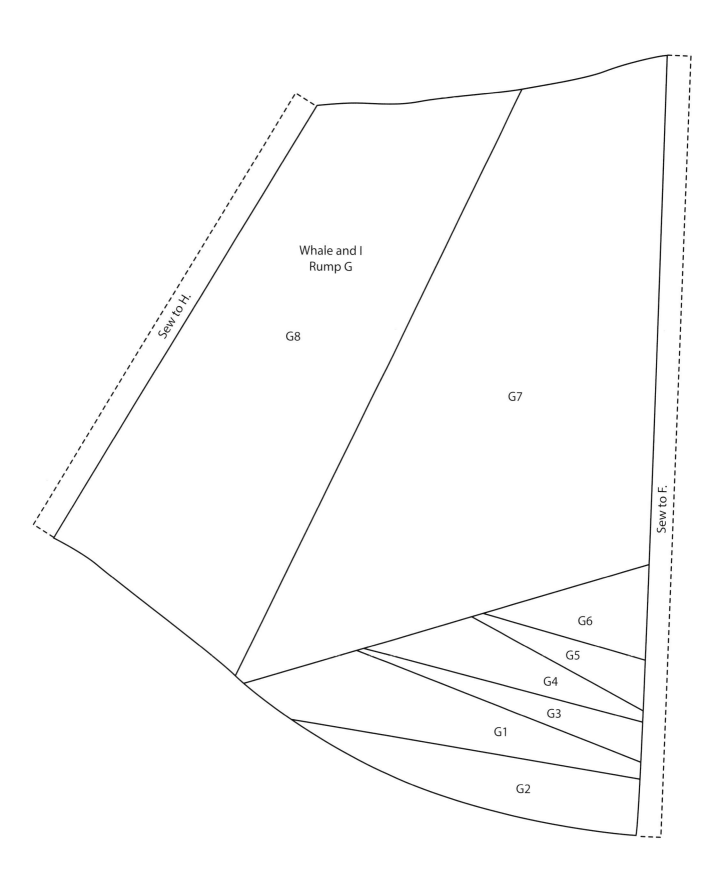

Whale and I
Rump G

Sew to H.

Sew to F.

G8

G7

G6

G5

G4

G3

G1

G2

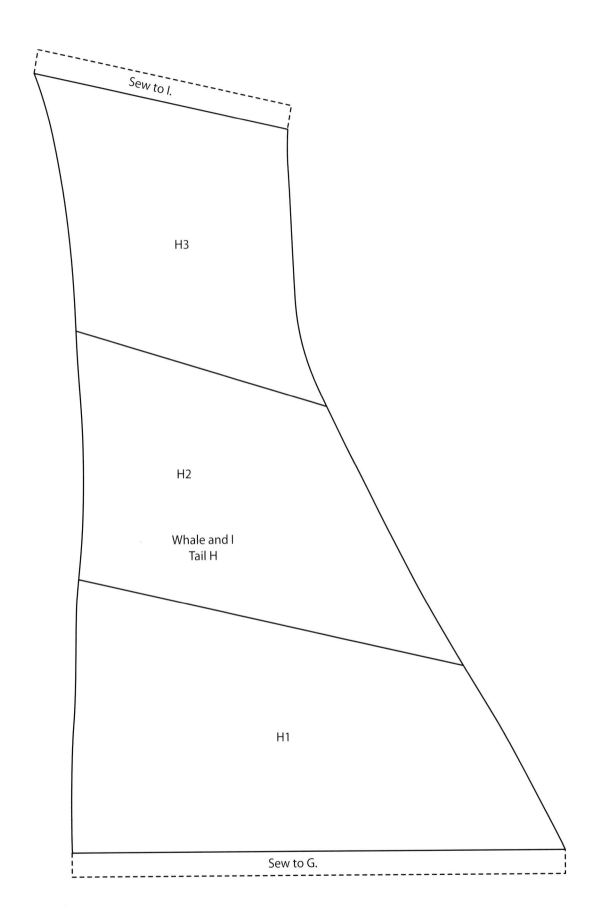

Sew to I.

H3

H2

Whale and I
Tail H

H1

Sew to G.

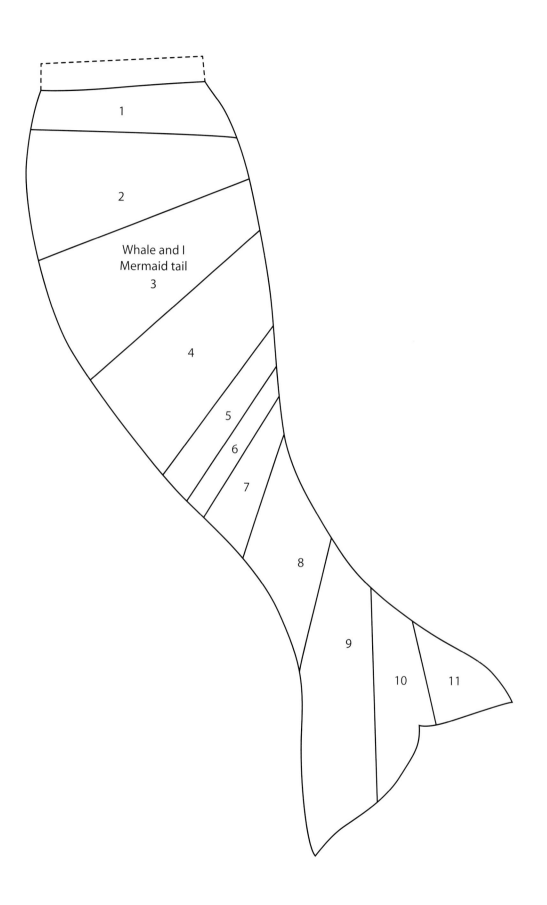

1

2

Whale and I
Mermaid tail

3

4

5

6

7

8

9

10

11

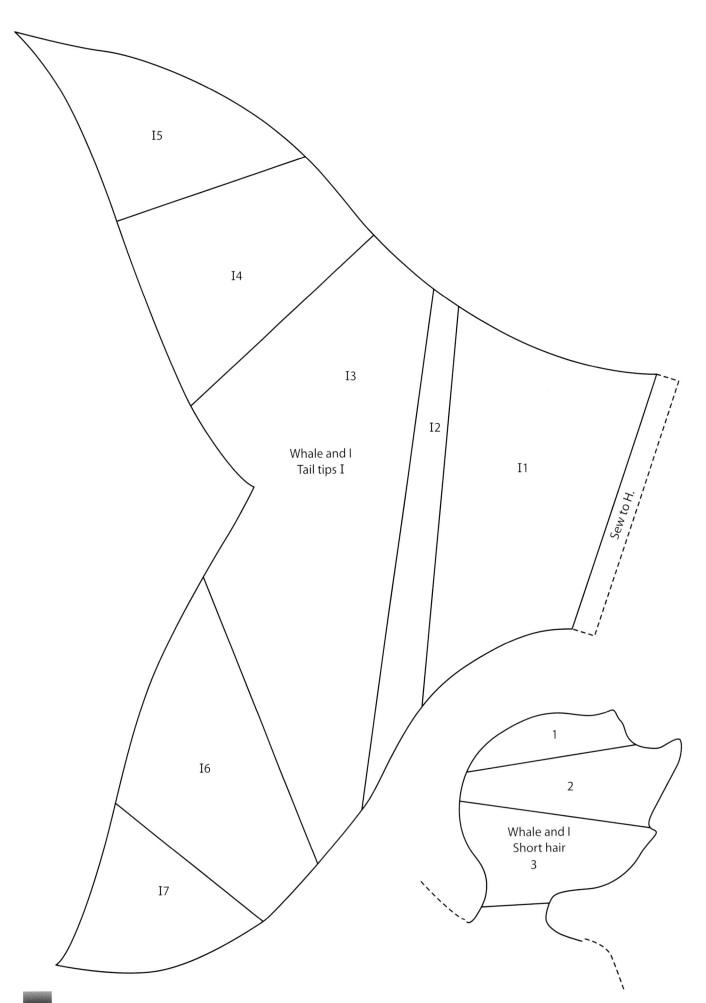

I5

I4

I3

Whale and I
Tail tips I

I2

I1

Sew to H.

I6

I7

1

2

Whale and I
Short hair
3

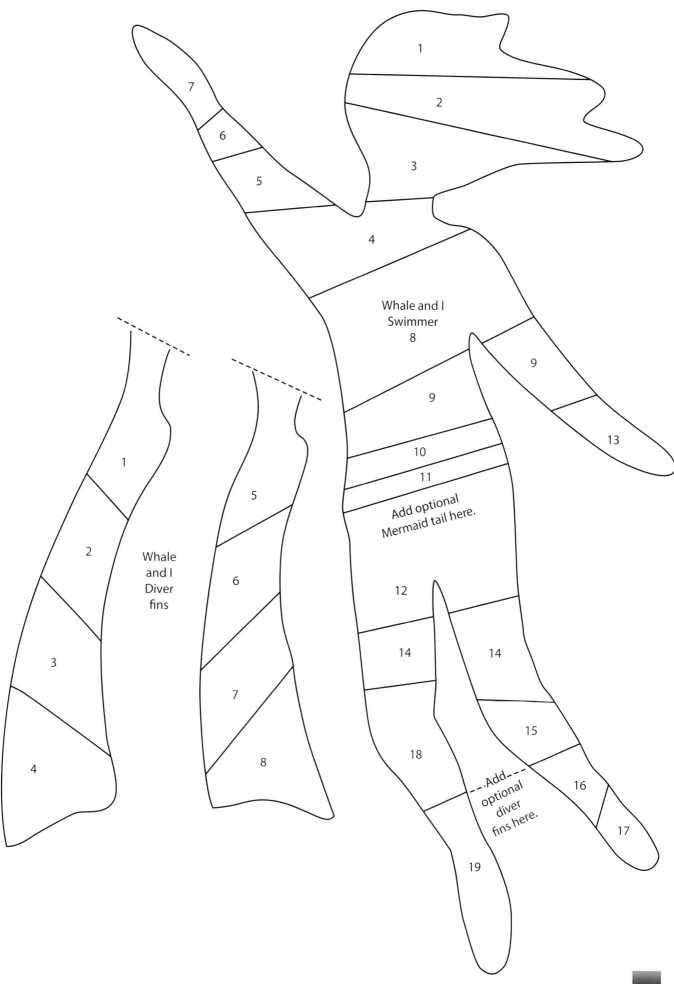

Dawn Star Quilt

Finished quilt: 60½″ × 60½″

Star quilts have been a favorite subject since I first experienced the Amish quilt collection of Esprit de Corps in downtown San Francisco in 1989. Achieving crisp, sharp points in stars and matching seams are skills you might want to master. You'll also gain a deeper understanding of color and value, as this quilt is inspired by the California sunrise in all its glory.

Pieced with assistance from Kristen Takakuwa, quilted by Jocelyn Marzan

MATERIALS

The more variety of shading in the ombrés, the better. This quilt incorporates color families predominately in various blue ombrés, with warm accents of yellows, pinks, and oranges. The following instructions give the total yardage needed to complete your quilt with some left over. Cut at least half of your required yardage first and organize the pieces based on color and value. This gives you options to pick and choose each block as you go. Enjoy playing with your expansive color palette!

Opal: 1½ yards

Cloud, Dawn, Evening, Haze, Heather, and Powder: 1 yard each

Ocean: ¾ yard

Mist: ¼ yard

Kona Cotton in Taupe: ¼ yard

Binding: ½ yard

Backing: 4 yards

Batting: 69″ × 69″

Opal   *Cloud*   *Dawn*   *Evening*   *Haze*

Heather   *Powder*   *Ocean*   *Mist*   *Kona Cotton in Taupe*

Photo by Jennifer Sampou

DESIGNING THE QUILT

Within each ombré fabric, the color work is done for you: light to dark, cool to warm, clear to muddy. All you need to do is systematically cut the pieces, arrange them on a table to see them all, and play on your design wall.

With this technique, there is no way you can go wrong. All the fabrics blend together and compliment each other. Do *at least* half of the cutting for the entire project before making one star. I suggest cutting all of it—this way you have the delightful, giddy freedom of creating with a chockablock full candy store of color.

This quilt has improv within structure, because some stars are missing distinguishable parts. This is my flexible way of designing. It gives you—the maker—permission to do all 25 blocks as double sawtooth stars (knock yourself out!) or just half if you want to leave a few points up to the imagination. The blank areas allow the ombré fabrics to breathe and bloom. And who can argue with that? If you are using monochromatic ombré fabric, you will need to add a few more choices to your selection to get that bursting thousand-colors-of-a-dawn-sky effect. Value is important—have the depth of the darkest of darks to the palest of lights. Refer to Value Study (page 36) for more information.

This is not meant to be a copycat quilt but a copycat technique. You create an assembly line of cutting and a table full of ombré fabric pieces. Your finished quilt will be different than mine yet capture the same spirit, just as the sunrise every day is never the same but the effect can be similar.

NUTS AND BOLTS OF 12″ BLOCKS

There are 25 blocks total: 5 large sawtooth stars, 6 small sawtooth stars with borders, and 14 double sawtooth stars, including 2 improv stars with the points left undone.

You have the freedom to mix and match the blocks as you like. It's fun to let the fabric speak to you, and with the way the pieces are cut, you can choose as you go along. Choose colors for the star and the background. Any and all fabrics serve as backgrounds and star colors. You mix and match the entire time based on value and a broad range of color palette.

I suggest making many of the 6″ stars first and then building on these, beginning with the yellow stars, which create the focus of the quilt. Notice that some stars are striking in contrast between light and dark and others are more quiet and closer in value.

This gives the quilt a dynamic and varied look. Quiet blocks support the more graphic "Look at me!" blocks. And it's what makes this quilt so interesting, soothing, and yet compelling. Also note that not all points of the star have to be the same colors. Have fun with your variety of star color and background color, which you can blend from star to star. Ombré is the style, so keep that in mind as your hues sway to and fro.

Star building with ombrés

TIP

I spent a bit more time blending the background colors together so the block-to-block transition was smooth. Eventually the background goes from pale to dark, while the stars bounce around in various hues, values, and contrasts. In order to capture this ombré effect of a rising sun, it is important to blend your blocks and play with placement.

Also, I didn't create the double sawtooth star right away. I kept my 6″ blocks separate from the 12″ blocks. I wanted the freedom to play and move them around. Take a snapshot and then walk out of the room and study the pictures you took. Come back with fresh eyes. This is a nuanced quilt; make sure to balance the eye-catching blocks with more quiet ones.

Ombré sky star layout

Photos by Jennifer Sampou

CUTTING

Cutting is based on 42" usable width of fabric (WOF). The cutting list below includes more pieces than needed for the 25 blocks. I want you to have plenty to play with as you arrange your stars.

Refer to this list for what 1 strip of fabric in varying widths will yield:

- 1 strip 6½" × WOF yields 6 squares 6½" × 6½" for the 12" star body.

- 1 strip 3½" × WOF yields 6 rectangles 3½" × 6½" for the 12" star background.

- 1 strip 3½" × WOF yields 12 squares 3½" × 3½" for the 6" star body, 12" star tips, and background corners.

- 1 strip 2" × WOF yields 12 rectangles 2" × 3½" for the 6" star background.

- 1 strip 2" × WOF yields 21 squares 2" × 2" for the 6" star tips and background corners.

Opal

- Cut 1 strip 6½" × WOF; subcut 6 squares 6½" × 6½".

- Cut 3 strips 3½" × WOF; subcut 18 rectangles 3½" × 6½".

- Cut 3 strips 3½" × WOF; subcut 36 squares 3½" × 3½".

- Cut 3 strips 2" × WOF; subcut 36 rectangles 2" × 3½".

- Cut 3 strips 2" × WOF; subcut 63 squares 2" × 2".

Cloud

- Cut 1 strip 6½" × WOF; subcut 6 squares 6½" × 6½".

- Cut 1 strip 3½" × WOF; subcut 6 rectangles 3½" × 6½".

- Cut 2 strips 3½" × WOF; subcut 24 squares 3½" × 3½".

Dawn

- Cut 2 strips 3½" × WOF; subcut 12 rectangles 3½" × 6½".

- Cut 3 strips 3½" × WOF; subcut 36 squares 3½" × 3½".

- Cut 2 strips 2" × WOF; subcut 42 squares 2" × 2".

Evening

- Cut 4 strips 3½" × WOF; subcut 24 rectangles 3½" × 6½".

- Cut 3 strips 3½" × WOF; subcut 36 squares 3½" × 3½".

- Cut 2 strips 2" × WOF; subcut 42 squares 2" × 2".

Haze

- Cut 4 strips 3½" × WOF; subcut 24 rectangles 3½" × 6½".

- Cut 3 strips 3½" × WOF; subcut 36 squares 3½" × 3½".

- Cut 2 strips 2" × WOF; subcut 24 rectangles 2" × 3½".

- Cut 1 strip 2" × WOF; subcut 21 squares 2" × 2".

Heather

- Cut 3 strips 3½" × WOF; subcut 18 rectangles 3½" × 6½".

- Cut 3 strips 3½" × WOF; subcut 36 squares 3½" × 3½".

- Cut 1 strip 2" × WOF; subcut 21 squares 2" × 2".

Powder

- Cut 1 strip 3½" × WOF; subcut 6 rectangles 3½" × 6½".

- Cut 3 strips 3½" × WOF; subcut 36 squares 3½" × 3½".

- Cut 2 strips 2" × WOF; subcut 24 rectangles 2" × 3½".

- Cut 1 strip 2" × WOF; subcut 21 squares 2" × 2".

Ocean

- Cut 1 strip 3½" × WOF; subcut 6 rectangles 3½" × 6½".

- Cut 3 strips 3½" × WOF; subcut 36 squares 3½" × 3½".

Mist

- Cut 1 strip 3½" × WOF; subcut 12 squares 3½" × 3½".

- Cut 1 strip 2" × WOF; subcut 21 squares 2" × 2".

Kona Cotton in Taupe

- Cut 1 strip 2" × WOF; subcut 12 rectangles 2" × 3½".

- Cut 1 strip 2" × WOF; subcut 21 squares 2" × 2".

CONSTRUCTION

Lay out your entire fabric palette. Arrange all of the shapes together in color families from light to dark.

Photo by Jennifer Sampou

Preparing the Star Points

Begin with your 4 yellow 6″ stars. Once you have made those, you will build your pale, light, medium, and dark blocks to surround and blend from there.

1. Lightly draw a diagonal line from corner to corner on the wrong sides of 2 star body 2″ × 2″ squares. Or, if you are confident (Go on—give it a try!), eyeball the diagonal stitch from point to point and forgo the marking. It's amazing how good we get with just a little practice.

2. With right sides together, place a square on the end of the 2″ × 3½″ rectangle.

3. Sew directly on the line, trim the seam allowance to ¼″, and press open.

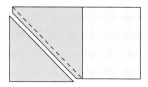 

4. With right sides together, place the other 2″ × 2″ square on the other end of the rectangle. Sew directly on the line, trim the seam allowance to ¼″, and press open.

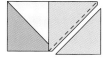 

Block Construction

1. Follow the diagram below for the piecing sequence. The arrows indicate which way to press. Look carefully where the tips intersect—it is important that they occur ¼″ in from the unfinished edge.

2. Sew the units together as shown. You want to see where the intersection is. Sew one hair to the right-hand side of the intersection; this allows for pressing. If the intersection has to be on the bottom and you cannot see it, mark the point with a pin.

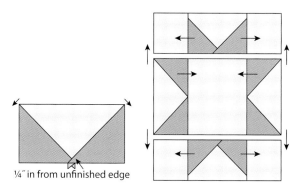

¼″ in from unfinished edge

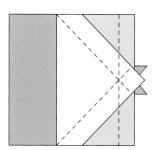 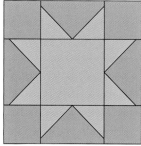

6″ Sawtooth Star with Borders

Follow the diagram below to add 3½″ × 3½″ squares and 3½″ × 6½″ rectangles to 6″ Sawtooth Stars.

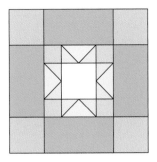

12″ Double Sawtooth Star

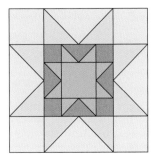

1. Follow Preparing the Star Points, Steps 1–4 (page 69), except use the 3½″ × 3½″ squares and the 3½″ × 6½″ rectangles.

2. Follow the diagram below for the piecing sequence. The arrows indicate which way to press.

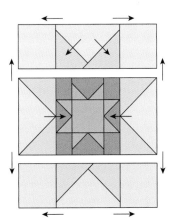

SETTING

1. Arrange your blocks from darks to lights to get the ombré effect across the quilt.

2. Sew the blocks into rows. Press the seams.

3. Sew the rows together. Press.

Finishing

Layer, baste, quilt, and bind using your favorite method.

About the Author

Curiosity. Nature. Design. Plus a huge dose of fun and love. These are what drive Jennifer Sampou's life.

Originally from Boston, Jennifer is the youngest of a large family of creatives. She studied surface design at the Fashion Institute of Technology in New York City and then got her feet wet at Laura Ashley in Wales as a young designer. Wanderlust led her to San Francisco, where she became the art director for P&B Textiles, putting them on the map in the early 90s as a dynamic cotton print house. Later, she opened Studio Sampou, licensing her designs to Robert Kaufman Fabrics. Jennifer has created thousands of best-selling fabrics, which have sold in the millions of yards. *Ombré Quilts* is her second book. She has written multiple patterns for C&T Publishing.

Traveling the world and living in Mexico and California have allowed Jennifer to keep her finger on the pulse, empowering her to remain fresh and bold as an ever-evolving artist. She loves to teach, lecture, and share her strong belief that everyone is creative. She feathers her nest in a small town outside San Francisco with her husband and three boys.

Seeing what people make with her fabrics brings her great joy because the creative process continues long after she's left her mark on a yard of fabric.

Visit Jennifer online and follow on social media!

Website: jennifersampou.com

Instagram: @jennifersampou

(Share your photos with the tag #jennifersampou!)

Pinterest: /jennifersampou

Facebook: /jennifersampou

BONUS VIDEOS ▶

Go to C&T Publishing's YouTube channel for video tutorials about paper piecing, machine appliqué, and using Jen's templates!

youtube.com/user/candtpublishing >

- search *Paper Piecing Tutorial*
- search *Choosing Colors for Appliqué*
- search *Professional-Looking Machine Appliqué Every Time*
- search *Jumbo Octagon Shimmer Templates Tutorial*

ALSO BY JENNIFER SAMPOU:

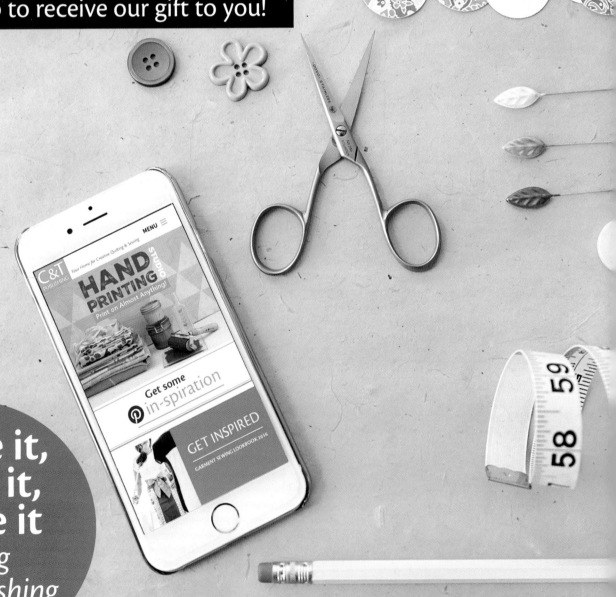

Want even more creative content?